A Clockwork Orange

✖ Controversies

Series editors: Stevie Simkin and Julian Petley

Controversies is a series comprising individual studies of controversial films from the late 1960s to the present day, encompassing classic, contemporary Hollywood, cult and world cinema. Each volume provides an in-depth study analyzing the various stages of each film's production, distribution, classification and reception, assessing both its impact at the time of its release and its subsequent legacy.

Also published

Neal King, *The Passion of the Christ*

Shaun Kimber, *Henry: Portrait of a Serial Killer*

Stevie Simkin, *Straw Dogs*

Forthcoming

Lucy Burke, *The Idiots*

Gabrielle Murray, *Bad Boy Bubby*

Jude Davies, *Falling Down*

Julian Petley, *Crash*

Stevie Simkin, *Basic Instinct*

'The *Controversies* series is a valuable contribution to the ongoing debate about what limits – if any – should be placed on cinema when it comes to the depiction and discussion of extreme subject matter. Sober, balanced and insightful where much debate on these matters has been hysterical, one-sided and unhelpful, these books should help us get a perspective on some of the thorniest films in the history of cinema.'
Kim Newman, novelist, critic and broadcaster

A Clockwork Orange

Peter Krämer

palgrave
macmillan

First published 2011 by
PALGRAVE MACMILLAN

Palgrave Macmillan in the UK is an imprint of Macmillan Publishers
Limited, registered in England, company number 785998, of Houndmills,
Basingstoke, Hampshire RG21 6XS.

Palgrave Macmillan in the US is a division of St Martin's Press LLC,
175 Fifth Avenue, New York, NY 10010.

Palgrave Macmillan is the global academic imprint of the above companies
and has companies and representatives throughout the world.

Palgrave® and Macmillan® are registered trademarks in the United States,
the United Kingdom, Europe and other countries

ISBN-13: 978–0–230–30212–9 paperback

This book is printed on paper suitable for recycling and made from fully
managed and sustained forest sources. Logging, pulping and
manufacturing processes are expected to conform to the environmental
regulations of the country of origin.

A catalogue record for this book is available from the British Library.

A catalog record for this book is available from the Library of Congress.

10   9   8   7   6   5   4   3   2   1
20   19   18   17   16   15   14   13   12   11

Printed in China

For Joe, Norbert and the Cinnamon Girl

Contents

Part 1: Key Themes and Ideas

Part 2: Key Scene Analysis

Part 3: Production History

Part 4: Marketing and Reception

Part 5: The Legacy of *A Clockwork Orange*

Appendices

Acknowledgements

The idea for this book came from Yoram Allon of Wallflower Press. I want to thank him for getting the project started. Many thanks are also due to the Leverhulme Trust, which granted me a one-year Leverhulme Research Fellowship award. Once again, staff at the Stanley Kubrick Archive in the Archive and Special Collections Centre at the University of the Arts London were immensely helpful. I also wish to thank the students on my final year undergraduate module 'Stanley Kubrick: Films in Context', who have shown a particular interest in, and have done a lot of excellent work on, *A Clockwork Orange* over the last few years. Last but not least, I want to thank Stevie Simkin and Joseph Garncarz for their extensive comments on the manuscript. In addition to his comments, Stevie has guided me masterfully through the difficult process of bringing this project to completion. I couldn't have done it without him!

✕ Introduction

On 21 January 1972, the *New York Times* reported that 'several dozen families in a plush, wooded section of Riverdale' in the Bronx had organised private security for their neighbourhood in response to the 'invasion of a neighbor's home by three armed, masked robbers who sexually assaulted a woman and her daughter' (Blumenthal, 1972, p. 48). The article noted that '[t]he attack … resembles somewhat the assaults by a band of hoodlums depicted in the film *A Clockwork Orange*'. This casual reference to the film (the only one in the article) indicates that, only four weeks after its initial release in the US, *A Clockwork Orange* had infiltrated public consciousness. Based on a British novel, and written, directed and produced in England by Stanley Kubrick, one of Hollywood's most critically acclaimed and most commercially successful filmmakers at that time, *A Clockwork Orange* had been declared one of the best films of 1971, while also performing well at the box office both in the US and in the UK where it had been released in mid-January. From the outset, it had been the target of vigorous attacks by some film reviewers and by other commentators. In subsequent months and years, the film's commercial performance would live up to the promise of the early weeks of its release, and the controversy it caused would further escalate, especially in the UK where the film was accused of being responsible for copycat crimes and banned by several local authorities. Indeed, Kubrick, who had been living in this country since the mid-1960s, was so troubled by the British controversy that, after *A Clockwork Orange* had completed its extremely long run in British cinemas, he asked the film's distributor, Warner Bros., not to show it again in the UK in his lifetime.

The *New York Times* article quoted above contains some clues as to how *A Clockwork Orange*, which featured two home invasions and rape as well as assorted other crimes, could have such an enormous impact. The article not only established a link between horrendous real-life crimes and particular film scenes, a link that would be explored in complex and contradictory ways in future debates about *A Clockwork Orange*, but also revealed a strong fascination with the nature of the crime itself and with the comprehensive threat posed by crimes of this kind. On the basis of an interview with the mother, the *New York Times* report described the attack on the Riverdale family in some detail: 'the doorbell rang at 8:45 P.M. When her 19-year-old son opened the door a crack to see who it was, a sawed-off shotgun was poked through.' Three men 'pushed their way into the 11-room house' and tied up both sons as well as '[a] sister of the mother who is paralyzed'. They 'were eager to establish' that '[t]he father was not yet home'. Holding a gun to her daughter's head, they forced the mother 'to guide them through the house', and grabbed 'pieces of jewelry and furs': 'Afterwards, the assailants ordered the mother and her daughter to an upstairs bedroom where the[y] abused them sexually.' Having tied up the women, they then took 'television sets and other property' out of the house. Police investigators observed that '[t]he family's description of the assailants tallied with descriptions of men involved in several other similar recent attacks near the city'. However, the mistakes the criminals made (such as leaving precious loot behind) suggested 'that they were more thrill-seekers than professional robbers'. The article concluded by noting that the police commissioner had 'sought to assure' Riverdale residents with the statement that 'arrests there for robbery and burglary were sharply up in 1971 over the preceding year'.

Here is America's newspaper of record assuming that its readers will want – or need – to know the details of this horrific attack, leaving only the precise nature of the sexual abuse of the two women to the imagination, but otherwise bringing the story to life with vivid descriptions. What is more, the events that readers are invited to participate in vicariously (mainly from the perspective of one of the victims) are not safely contained and distanced; instead readers are reminded that such attacks take place with some regularity all over the New York metropolitan area. Indeed, the police commissioner's assurance that arrest rates are up is double-edged: Perhaps they have increased not because of greater police efforts but because more robberies and burglaries are being committed. This would appear to be the interpretation favoured by Riverdale residents who do not feel protected sufficiently by the police and instead organise their own security. In this way the article suggests a potential threat to everyone. Even the majority of readers who do not live in huge houses in 'plush' neighbourhoods, with all the trappings of affluence, are not safe, because the home invaders do not appear to be professionals mainly interested in material goods, but thrill-seekers who enjoy threatening people and exerting power over them, culminating in sexual abuse. Everyone, irrespective of their wealth, could be the next target for such a gang, women especially.

It is precisely such a comprehensive threat that is staged in a sexually explicit and graphically violent, but also highly stylised and in places sickly comical fashion in *A Clockwork Orange*. The film portrays a society of the near future, in which the nights appear to be dominated by roving gangs of teenage males who beat people up in the streets and in the houses they invade, while also engaging in vicious fights with each other; who steal whatever they can lay their hands on, rape women both in their homes and outside of them, and also kill people. Unlike the above article, on the whole the film invites – one might even say forces – viewers to experience all of this criminal behaviour mainly from the perspective of the perpetrators, rather than from that of their victims. The film starts with a tight close-up of the leader of one of the gangs, Alex, who is also speaking the voiceover narration – using a very peculiar slang – and who appears in every scene, indeed in most shots; first and foremost this is *his* story, and not that of his victims.

Interestingly, though, in the film's two home-invasion scenes – both of which involve grand houses, surrounded by trees, far away from the city centre – there are moments which foreground the experiences and perspectives of those at the receiving end of the violence. In the first home-invasion scene, it is the point of view of the male victim that is foregrounded. Alex and the other three masked members of his gang first beat him up, and then make him watch while his wife is sexually assaulted by Alex, the film cutting back and forth between shots of the husband's horrified face and reverse shots showing the attack on his wife as seen from his perspective. The second scene features a middle-aged woman who gets suspicious when Alex tries to talk her into opening her door because she has heard the news about the previous night's attack. During her phone call to the police, Alex is off screen for much longer than is usual in this film, and when he finally appears and gets into a fight with the woman, there are several shots reproducing her movements and perspective, right up to the moment when he rams the sculpture of a giant phallus in her face (figs. 1–2).

Thus there are numerous parallels between the film scenes and the *New York Times* crime report in which they are referenced: the 'wooded' location of the houses being invaded, the apparent wealth of their inhabitants, the small group of masked intruders, the emphasis on sex and violence rather than theft (it remains unclear what the gang steals during the film's first home invasion, and Alex definitely does not take anything during the second). In terms of perspective, the fact that the article is based on an interview with the mother – including a direct quotation from her – strangely echoes the film's emphasis on the dialogue and experiences of the middle-aged woman in the second home-invasion scene. Even more intriguingly, the *New York Times* article foregrounds the fact that the invaders were 'eager' to ascertain that the father was not at home, which implies that his presence might have been enough to deter them, and also, perhaps, raises the question of how *he* might feel about what happened to his family, in particular about his failure to prevent the assault. The first home-invasion scene in *A Clockwork Orange* certainly focuses on the husband's experience in this way and in later scenes, the film returns to the devastating effect the attack itself and the subsequent death of his wife have had on him.

When the *New York Times* reporter referred to *A Clockwork Orange*, he undoubtedly did not have such close comparative analysis in mind. Instead, it would appear that he merely wanted to evoke the two home-invasion scenes so that those readers who had seen the film could replay them in their minds

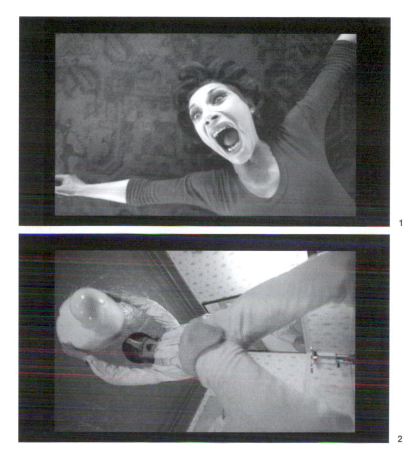

1

2

while reading the account of the attack in Riverdale. In particular, memory of the film's highly sexualised attacks on women could fill in the blank the article left. Two days after the *New York Times* article used *A Clockwork Orange* in this merely illustrative fashion, a popular and more downmarket British paper, the *Sunday People*, foregrounded the film in its report about the Riverdale incident. Under the title 'Hunt for *Clockwork Orange* Sex Gang', the article opened with the claim that the Riverdale criminals 'have modelled themselves on the rape-and-robbery hoodlums in the film *A Clockwork Orange*' (Blyth, 1972). A list of several details shared by the real-life crime and the filmic crime followed, among them the following: Before the home invaders 'forced their way' into the house, '[l]ike the teenage "Droogs" in Stanley Kubrick's controversial picture they pretend there has been an accident' and ask whether they can come in '"to phone for an ambulance"'; and before they 'raped' mother and daughter, '[a]s in the picture they first cut off their victims' clothes'. The report concluded with a quotation from a police officer: 'The similarities with the *Clockwork Orange* gang are uncanny.' Although nothing was in fact known about the attackers, the article invited its readers to conclude that they must have seen the film and then copied some of the crimes depicted in it.

Apart from the concluding quotation and the remarkable – indeed rather unlikely – similarities between crime and film, the information presented in this article is the same as that in the *New York Times* report, and it is doubtful that the *Sunday People* writer did conduct much, or indeed any, additional research; in other words, the new information provided in this article would appear to be the result of wishful thinking. What is not in doubt, however, is that the *Sunday People* first of all judged the news value of the film, which had been released in the UK ten days earlier, to be very high, and was also confident that, even without any but the most indirect evidence, readers would accept the claim that such a film could in effect cause people to commit certain kinds of crimes. Perhaps it was the disturbing nature of the crime and the absence of detailed information about the criminals that opened up a space for this claim. The home invaders were not simply pursuing material gain, but were – in the words of both the *New York Times* and the *Sunday People* – 'thrill-seekers' who are stimulated by danger and power as well as physical and sexual violence. Indeed by describing the criminals as a 'sex gang' in its headline, the *Sunday People* article suggested that ultimately some kind of sexual stimulation and release was their main objective.

Explaining why people pursue such stimulation and release through brutal crimes is in many ways more difficult than accounting for crimes motivated by material needs or greed, or by emotions such as jealousy and anger erupting in a particular situation. Hence, it is tempting for anyone confronted with such crimes to speculate about more unorthodox causes. Given the popularity of and public debate about *A Clockwork Orange* at the time of the report about the Riverdale incident, it is understandable that the thrill-seeking behaviour of the film's young criminals would have entered the reporter's thoughts, as well as the thrills that the film might provide an audience. There is a certain logic if one then speculates that, having experienced the protagonist's pleasures vicariously, criminal viewers might well be encouraged to adjust their crimes along the lines suggested by the film; indeed, it would be possible to conclude that even viewers without a criminal history might be tempted to replicate – and intensify – their experience in the cinema by acting out the film's fictional scenarios for real. This is the kind of reasoning underpinning the *Sunday People* article; indeed it is the kind of reasoning that readers might apply to the report in the *New York Times*, which in itself does not mention a causal link between the film and the crime, but contains all the elements, which could invite such a conclusion.

In different ways, then, the articles in the *New York Times* and the *Sunday People* indicate that the high-profile release of *A Clockwork Orange* in the US and the UK made the film a natural reference point in press reports and public debates about crime waves and thrill-seeking behaviour, whereby it could be used for illustrative or for explanatory purposes. Such usage in turn gave the film an ever-higher profile, generating increased interest on the part of movie audiences and film critics and drawing ever more people into the continuing discussion about *A Clockwork Orange*. Importantly, these people included British author Anthony Burgess on whose 1962 novel of the same title the film was based. On 28 January 1972, only five days after the *Sunday People* article and directly referencing its headline, the London *Evening News* featured an article based on an interview with Burgess, entitled '*Clockwork Orange* Gang Killed My Wife' (Hall, 1972, p. 10). The novelist revealed that *A Clockwork Orange* had been inspired by a wartime incident, in which four American deserters had attacked his first wife, then pregnant, in London; she subsequently 'had to have an abortion because of shock', never fully recovered from the trauma and died at the age of forty in 1968. This revelation placed the couple whose house is invaded in both novel and film at the centre of the story, rather than Alex and his gang. In this perspective, the story is about the victims' suffering rather than the perpetrators' thrills, and, for the author, it was meant to be a way to replay and thus, hopefully, to work through personal trauma: 'I had to get this damn thing out of my system. I wrote the scene where a writer and his wife are attacked. … the house they live in is called "home". That's how strongly I felt.'

When asked whether the film could 'incite teenage louts into orgies of rape and destruction', Burgess responded: 'I don't think anyone will go out and beat up little old ladies after seeing it unless they are going to do so anyway.' He also stated that '[m]an is basically evil, anyway … we are all essentially aggressive and will never be anything different'. Yet, he pointed out, '[t]he whole point of the book and the film is: It's better to do wrong of your own free will than to do right because the state ordains it.' Here he referred to what happens to Alex in the story once he is captured by the police (after about a third of the film's running time). In prison he volunteers for an innovative medical treatment that can get him out early because it will prevent him from committing further violent crimes; it is an aversion therapy which combines the injection of drugs with the screening of violent films. After the treatment he is set free, unable to defend himself when he encounters his former victims who want to take revenge and eventually drive him to a suicide attempt. He ends up in hospital where he realises that the aversion therapy is no longer effective; he is able to return to his old way of life.

Burgess insisted not only that novel and film were meant to show that the treatment was worse than the crimes Alex had committed, but that the 'aggressive urge' was 'curiously cognate with the creative urge', thus suggesting that the state's suppression of violence would also kill art, perhaps even that there was something of an artist in Alex. This is surely a remarkable stance to take for a writer who said that he had created Alex in order to work through the impact of the devastating attack on his wife by people much like Alex; in fact, Burgess's remark would seem to establish a close connection between his own 'creative urge' and Alex's 'aggressive urge'. In an article Burgess published in the *Los Angeles Times* two weeks later, he put his argument in an explicitly religious framework, stating that the novel 'was intended to be a sort of tract, even a sermon'; and its message was: 'The wish to diminish free will is ... [a] sin against the Holy Ghost' (Burgess, 1972, pp. 1, 18). With regards to the attack on his wife and what he admitted to be the surprisingly appealing characterisation of Alex in the story, he wrote: 'The point is that, if we are going to love mankind, we will have to love Alex as a not unrepresentative member of it' (p. 19); this also implied that he himself – through the creative act of writing a novel – learnt to love his late wife's attackers.

Burgess's provocative statements about *A Clockwork Orange* at the time of the film's initial release suggest that it is worth taking a closer look at the origins as well as the style and content of his novel, which – in addition to situating the film in Stanley Kubrick's career and examining the adaptation process – I do in Part 3 of this book, before exploring the marketing and reception of *A Clockwork Orange* in the US and the UK (in Part 4) as well as the film's legacy (in Part 5). Before conducting this examination of the film's production and reception contexts, I analyse the film's main themes (in Part 1) and key scenes (in Part 2), including the first home invasion. In the remainder of this Introduction, I want to preface my discussion of *A Clockwork Orange* with some remarks on my personal engagement with the film as well as on academic debates and historical developments, which are relevant for this study.

I first saw *A Clockwork Orange* as a teenager in Germany in the late 1970s, and without knowing much – or indeed anything – about the controversy surrounding the film, I was so excited and intrigued that I also read Burgess's novel, which in turn became the focus of what was probably the first extended critical essay that I ever wrote in my life (as an assignment for my German class). I was mainly interested in the criminal violence so central to the story, and how its representation in novel and film had such different effects on me. Frankly, in addition to being shocked and disturbed, I had found the first third of the film very exhilarating, which was probably the main reason for my repeat viewings of *A Clockwork Orange* over the next few years. By contrast, when reading the novel, which is a first-person narrative told in Alex's peculiar slang, I found it very difficult to make out what exactly was happening; indeed, the inventiveness of the language was more exciting than the action that was being relayed with it. In my school essay, I argued that the book's language not only distances the reader from Alex's brutality, thus making identification with him less objectionable, but also both expresses and enhances Alex's distance from his own actions, in particular from their impact on his victims. The language Alex speaks and thinks in allows him to disregard the suffering of others (and also, later in the novel, his own suffering at the hands of others) while simultaneously intensifying his enjoyment of his mocking, abusive, violent behaviour. At the heart of my initial encounters with *A Clockwork Orange*, novel and film, then, was the question of how people like Alex were able to behave the way they did, and a concern about my own willingness, indeed eagerness, to enjoy such behaviour vicariously in the cinema.

There is, of course, a richly diverse literature, in the disciplines of anthropology, psychology, sociology, criminology, philosophy and biology, on the kind of excessive violence exemplified by Alex's crimes in the film and, to a lesser extent, by those of the home invaders in Riverdale: apparently unmotivated (at least as far as familiar motives such as greed, self-defence, revenge etc. are concerned), remorseless, extreme in its execution, intended both physically to damage and to humiliate victims, whereby such damage and humiliation serve no other end than to provide the perpetrator with sensual thrills and a sense of power.[1] It might be a productive exercise to compare the film's depiction of Alex's crimes, and the explanations for his behaviour which the film could be said to imply, with the scholarly literature on this topic, to determine whether the film offers an adequate or a heavily mythologised account, but also perhaps to explore whether it has something original to say about the matter. But this is not one of the objectives of this book.

Nevertheless, I think it is worth noting that, if we disregard the excessiveness of the young criminals' behaviour, the opening third of

A Clockwork Orange would appear to be very much in line with the 'general theory of crime' proposed by the criminologists Michael R. Gottfredson and Travis Hirschi. On the basis of an extensive review of the literature and of crime statistics, they note that 'crime is heavily concentrated among the young' (Gottfredson and Hirschi, 1990, p. xiv), that the vast majority of crime is committed by males (pp. 145–6), and that the main cause of crime is lack of self-control in those who engage in criminal activity, combined with the weakness of external restraints:

> Crime does not require deprivation, peer influence, or the gang; it says little about one's biological past and is in no way akin to work. It requires no planning or skill, and 'careers' in crime go nowhere but down. Nearly all crimes are mundane, simple, trivial, easy acts aimed at satisfying desires of the moment. … [T]he offender appears to have little control over his or her own desires. When such desires conflict with long-term interests, those lacking self-control opt for the desires of the moment, whereas those with greater self-control are governed by the restraints imposed by the consequences of acts displeasing to family, friends, and the law. (p. xv)

The scholarly literature on crime rarely, if ever, offers in-depth discussions of the influence of film or other modern media and cultural forms on criminals, presumably because their influence is considered to be rather weak in comparison to other causal factors. Curiously, though, a significant proportion of scholarly work on the media is concerned with the possible negative effects that they might have on their audiences, in particular by causing, or at least enhancing, deviant, criminal and violent dispositions and behaviour. With regards to cinema, such work goes as far back as the 1910s (Grieveson, 2008). Relating to a range of media and cultural forms (including comic books and television), it reached a high point – and garnered considerable publicity – both in the US and the UK in the 1950s (Barker, 1984a; Gilbert, 1986; Beaty, 2005) and also, as I will discuss later, in the late

1960s and early 1970s. The scholarly literature in what has become known as the 'media- effects tradition' is vast.[2] It has in turn been the subject of extensive philosophical reflections as well as political and methodological critiques.[3]

I should point out that it is not the aim of this book to determine the (possible, probable or actual) 'effects' of *A Clockwork Orange* on its viewers. I find the concern about how viewers deal with representations of violence in the cinema to be perfectly understandable; indeed, as mentioned earlier, my initial encounters with *A Clockwork Orange* and similar films led me to become conscious of, and worried about, my own enjoyment of on-screen violence. However, as should be obvious from my earlier comments on the *Sunday People* report about the Riverdale incident, I am extremely sceptical about claims that the film had a direct and decisive influence on people's criminal behaviour. While in principle this is possible, newspaper reports alleging such influence either present no evidence whatsoever, or, as is the case with the article in the *Sunday People*, are based on claims about similarities between a film scene and a crime, which are less than compelling; such similarities are mostly far too vague, or, alternatively, suspiciously precise. Certainly, research on the audiences of *A Clockwork Orange* (to be discussed in Part 5), as well as other studies, which use interviews and focus-group discussions to examine the ways in which viewers engage with various forms of violent entertainment,[4] demonstrate that people watch films featuring violence for a range of reasons and in a wide variety of circumstances, and that their sensual, emotional, moral and intellectual responses to these films are complex and varied.

If we want to understand how and why such complexity and variation is replaced in much public commentary, such as the article in the *Sunday People*, by simplistic ideas about films causing crime, and also how and why claims about the nefarious influence of cinema and other media can escalate and multiply at particular historical moments, we can turn to the sociological literature on the social construction of social problems and on so-called 'moral panics'.[5] This literature reveals a process whereby certain interest groups, often professionals (such as physicians or social workers) close to a particular social phenomenon (e.g., adults inflicting harm on children), make claims about the immense destructiveness and widespread prevalence of this phenomenon, these claims being picked up and widely circulated by the media; the aim of such campaigning is to generate support and resources for the professional group in question so as to enable it to deal more effectively with this now widely recognised phenomenon and also, in many cases, to bring about new legislation and stricter law-enforcement. Importantly, this basic process is the same whether one deals with what on reflection may be regarded as legitimate social problems, or with so-called 'moral panics', which are judged to make vastly exaggerated claims about the problem at hand.

As it turns out, much of the scholarly literature on the construction of social problems and on moral panics deals with public debates about violent crime, in particular where it has – or is assumed to have – a sexual dimension.[6] There are also numerous studies of debates about the alleged role of mass media and popular culture in causing crime or, more generally, on their assumed negative impact on the morality and emotional stability of audiences.[7] It is worth noting that, while in debates about media effects and violent crime, young children feature prominently as victims, adolescents and young adults, especially males, are often focused on as perpetrators, and it is frequently claimed that their delinquent behaviour is caused by their exposure to the harmful influence of mass media and popular culture.[8] These debates form the backdrop for the controversy surrounding *A Clockwork Orange*. While I would not wish to go as far as to claim that this controversy amounted to a 'moral panic', it is certainly the case that it was informed by the kinds of claims that social-problem discourses and moral panics about youth, (sex) crime and the media had made across previous decades, especially claims about the power of media to move people, notably impressionable youth, so deeply that they committed crimes that they would not otherwise have committed.

Stanley Kubrick certainly acknowledged the seductive power his film – and in particular its protagonist – was to exert over the audience. In an interview six months before the film's release he talked about his intention to move viewers at a deep emotional level:

> The emotions of people are far more similar than their intellects. The common bond is their subconscious emotional reaction. ... I use Alex to explore an aspect of the human personality. He does things which one knows are wrong, and yet you find yourself being taken in by him and accepting his frame of reference. As in a dream, the film demands a suspension of moral judgment. (Hofsess, 1971/2001, pp. 106–7)

Such statements about viewers sharing Alex's experiences and perspective without considering their moral dimension must have been worrying for people who believed that films could stimulate criminal behaviour. Yet, while agreeing to his interviewers' suggestion that 'violent behaviour will be a growing problem in the future' and also acknowledging 'an accelerating erosion of any kind of mystique which authority may have once had, and an over-awareness of the romantic concept of rebellion', Kubrick insisted that it was important 'to appreciate the realities of a complex society', the very realities his film dealt with (p. 107). At the same time, he pointed out that he did not see *A Clockwork Orange* 'as being primarily or even significantly, a topical, social story', but as dealing more generally with human nature (p. 107). He admitted that (much like Anthony Burgess) he had what could be regarded as a rather negative view of this nature – '[w]e are such rapacious creatures' – yet saw the impetus behind his films, in particular the darkly comic *A Clockwork Orange*, as basically optimistic: 'A satirist is someone who has a very skeptical, pessimistic view of human nature ... but who still has the optimism to make some sort of joke out of it. However brutal that joke might be' (p. 107). Without saying so directly, Kubrick implied that the detachment and awareness which comic exaggeration could give rise to might help people to change their ways. Let's take a closer look, then, at Kubrick's satire.

✕ Synopsis

As is the case with many other Kubrick films, *A Clockwork Orange* is in some ways a highly ambiguous film, not only in terms of what its 'message' might be, but also in terms of what is actually happening in the film. Any summary of the story should, I think, acknowledge such basic ambiguities, rather than resolving them one way or the other. Hence the following synopsis only makes use of information provided by the film itself, rather than pieces of information we may derive from the novel or from the many interviews that Anthony Burgess and Stanley Kubrick have given about *A Clockwork Orange*. In addition, I want to capture how the story gradually unfolds and thus to approximate the way in which audiences may piece together the story upon their first viewing of the film. So as to give a better sense of the film's structure, I have numbered individual scenes and provided the start time of each scene (I will refer back to these in Parts 1–2).* So here goes:

---

* For a slightly different way of segmenting the films into scenes, see Falsetto, 2001, pp. 183–5. I should point out that both this synopsis and my analysis of *A Clockwork Orange* were helped by Kubrick's illustrated book about the film, which reproduces frames from most shots as well as the dialogue and the voiceover narration (Kubrick, 1972/2000). For timing purposes, I have used the American DVD, which reproduces the film at the same speed as it was shown in the cinema (twenty-four frames per second), whereas the British DVD, reproduces the film at twenty-five frames per second. The timings for the British version are: Scene 1, 0:42; Scene 2, 2:10; Scene 3, 4:16; Scene 4, 7:12; Scene 5, 8:35; Scene 6, 12:48; Scene 7, 16:04; Scene 8, 16:57; Scene 9, 19:12; Scene 10, 20:39; Scene 11, 24:43; Scene 12, 26:55; Scene 13, 27:52; Scene 14, 31:56; Scene 15, 33:36; Scene 16, 35:00; Scene 17, 41:44; Scene 18, 45:23; Scene 19,

After the film's minimalist credit sequence, the story begins with a tight close-up of a young man staring at the camera (Scene 1, 0:43) who, in voiceover narration, introduces himself as Alex. He and his 'droogs' Georgie, Dim and Pete drink milk which is spiked with something that prepares them 'for a bit of the old ultra-violence'. The film cuts to a night scene (2, 2:15): a drunk and dishevelled old man lies on the ground in an underpass. Alex and his droogs approach him, mock him and beat him up. The next scene (3, 4:26) initially focuses on the stage of an abandoned theatre, on which five young men are sexually assaulting a young woman. Alex and his droogs interrupt proceedings by challenging the other gang to a fight, which they win, before running off at the sound of police sirens. Next (Scene 4, 7:30) we see Alex, surrounded by his droogs, at the steering wheel of a car, racing along a country lane and forcing other cars off the road. Alex's voiceover announces 'the old surprise visit' at a house called 'Home'. The car stops in front of the house (Scene 5, 8:56) and the gang sneaks up on it. When Alex rings the bell, the woman of the house initially refuses to let him in, until the man of the house tells her to open the door. Wearing masks, Alex and his droogs invade the house, beating the man down to the ground (with Alex performing 'Singin' in the Rain') and then encouraging him to watch while Alex sexually assaults his wife. Next (Scene 6, 13:20) we see Alex and his droogs arriving back at the Korova Milk Bar. When a woman starts singing the 'Ode to Joy' from Beethoven's *Ninth Symphony*, Alex's great enjoyment of this is disrupted by Dim who makes a rude noise, for which Alex hits him. Alex is then (Scene 7, 16:45) seen walking across a concrete cityscape towards a block of flats where he lives with his 'dadda and mum'. In his parents' flat (Scene 8, 17:40), Alex

---

50:45; Scene 20, 52:13; Scene 21, 58:48; Scene 22, 62:25; Scene 23, 64:34; Scene 24, 66:56; Scene 25, 68:17; Scene 26, 71:32; Scene 27, 72:27; Scene 28, 76:00; Scene 29, 84:31; Scene 30, 91:58; Scene 31, 95:25; Scene 32, 98:10; Scene 33, 102:23; Scene 34, 105:05; Scene 35, 113:16; Scene 36, 116:11; Scene 37, 117:16; Scene 38, 117:43; Scene 39, 118:57; Scene 40, 122:22; beginning of end credits, 128:26; end of credits, 130:58.

goes to the toilet before retiring to his bed to listen to Beethoven's *Ninth Symphony* while imagining violent scenes.

The next morning (Scene 9, 20:00), he tells his mother that he cannot go to school because he does not feel well. When Alex later leaves his room (Scene 10, 21:30), he finds his 'Post Corrective Adviser' Mr Deltoid sitting on his parents' bed, questioning him about the events of the previous night. Afterwards (Scene 11, 25:45), Alex picks up two young women in a record shop, and has sex with them in his room (Scene 12, 28:02). In the lobby of his block of flats (Scene 13, 29:01), he is surprised to find his droogs. Georgie and Dim want to introduce 'a new way' for running the gang, which includes making more money. Outside (Scene 14, 33:16), Alex beats up the two rebels to reassert his authority, but in the Duke of New York pub (Scene 15, 35:00) he then agrees to carry out Georgie's plan, which is to rob a 'health farm' currently occupied by a lone woman. Next (Scene 16, 36:27), we see the woman (identified as 'Catlady' in the credits) exercising and then refusing entry to Alex. While, her suspicions aroused, she calls the police, Alex enters the house through an upstairs window. Wearing his mask, he confronts her and she attacks him with a Beethoven bust. The fight ends with Alex ramming a phallus sculpture into her face. When he hears a police siren, he exits the house. Outside, Dim hits Alex in the face with a milk bottle and he goes to the ground. Alex is next (Scene 17, 43:28) seen in a bare room, being questioned by three policemen. Mr Deltoid joins them, revealing that the woman Alex attacked has died, and spitting in Alex's face.

The next scene (18, 47:17) opens with aerial shots introducing the prison, which Alex enters, having been 'sentenced to 14 years'. He is processed by several guards, stripped and given a rectal exam. The film cuts to a close-up of a chaplain (Scene 19, 52:52), delivering a passionate sermon. The film then shows Alex in the prison library (Scene 20, 55:26). Alex's voiceover reveals that he has been in prison for two years, assisting the chaplain. He studies the Bible and imagines various violent and sexual scenes. He asks the chaplain about 'this new treatment that gets you out of prison in no time at all'. The chaplain, referring to the importance of free will, is sceptical about the

'Ludovico Technique'. Next (Scene 21, 61:15), Alex is seen walking around in circles among other prisoners in the prison courtyard. A middle-aged man is shown the facilities, talking about the government's plans to 'kill the criminal reflex' in prisoners. When Alex speaks up, the man picks him: 'This vicious young hoodlum will be transformed out of all recognition.' Next (Scene 22, 65:00), Alex enters the office of the prison governor, who tells him that the man he met earlier was the 'new Minister of the Interior'. The Minister has decided that Alex 'will be transferred to the Ludovico Medical Facility' for treatment, which should allow him to 'leave state custody in a little over a fortnight'. Alex signs some papers.

In the following scene (23, 67:15) the chief guard delivers him to the Ludovico facility. Next (Scene 24, 69:44) we see a female doctor entering the room where Alex is resting in bed. She introduces herself as Dr Branom, the assistant of Dr Brodsky, who is in charge of Alex's treatment. She gives him an injection and announces that 'we're just going to show you some films'. The film cuts to a largely empty cinema auditorium (Scene 25, 71:08). Medical personnel sit at the back, while at the front Alex is strapped into a seat and a headrest, his eyes being forced open by clamps. The violent films he is shown make him sick. Dr Brodsky explains that this is due to the drug given to Alex. Back in bed in his room (Scene 26, 74:31), Alex talks to Dr Branom about the first viewing session; she explains that his getting sick is a sign that he is getting better. The film cuts to documentary images of a Nazi rally (Scene 27, 75:28) and of war scenes. When Alex realises that the screening is accompanied by Beethoven's *Ninth Symphony*, he protests loudly. Alex shouts that he has learnt his lesson, but Dr Brodsky insists that the treatment has to go on. Next we see Alex walking onto a stage (Scene 28, 79:10), being introduced to an audience including the chief guard, the prison chaplain and Drs Brodsky and Branom by the Minister of the Interior. He declares that his party's promise 'to restore law and order … is now about to become a reality'. On stage, Alex is abused by a man, verbally and physically. Lying on the ground, Alex responds to the sickness he feels by licking the man's shoe. After a round of applause, a young woman approaches Alex, naked but for her panties. He reaches out for her, and then gets violently sick once more. The audience applauds again, and the minister joins Alex on stage, explaining that 'the intention to act violently is accompanied by strong feelings of physical distress. To counter these, the subject has to switch to a diametrically opposed attitude.' The prison chaplain objects that Alex has 'no real choice'. The minister insists that 'the point is that it works'.

The next scene (29, 88:02) starts with Alex entering his parents' flat. They are surprised to see him and nervous because they have rented out his room to a young man named Joe. Joe accuses Alex of having treated his parents badly; Alex tries to hit him and gets sick immediately. A distraught Alex leaves, and his mother starts crying. The film cuts to Alex walking along a river embankment (Scene 30, 95:48) and staring pensively into the water. The drunk from the film's opening approaches him to ask for money, which Alex gives to him. Only then does the man recognise him, and while Alex quickly gets sick again, he is dragged to an underpass where a crowd of old people attacks him. Two policemen disperse the crowd. When Alex looks up, he recognises them as Dim and Georgie. The next scene (31, 99:23) shows a car driving in a forest. Dim and Georgie drag Alex to a trough, beat him and half-drown him. Then they leave. The film cuts to a nighttime scene (32, 102:15); Alex stumbles around in heavy rain, arriving at the house he previously invaded. We see the man of the house (Frank Alexander) and, in place of the woman in the earlier scene, there is now a huge, muscular man (Julian), who lets Alex into the house. While Alex realises where he is, the wheelchair-bound Frank does not recognise him as his attacker. However, he knows from press reports that Alex is 'the poor victim of this horrible new technique'. Next (Scene 33, 106:39), Alex is taking a bath, while Frank calls political allies, proposing to use Alex as a 'potent weapon … to ensure that the government is not returned in the forthcoming election'. Alex has meanwhile started singing 'Singin' in the Rain', and, hearing this, a truly horrified look appears on Frank's face. We next (Scene 34: 109:28) see Alex sitting at the dining-room table, eating spaghetti. Frank and Julian join him. The obviously distressed Frank pushes some wine on the suspicious Alex and then talks about his dead wife; while 'the doctors told me it was pneumonia', he believes Alex's attack on her to be responsible for her death. A man and a woman, who Frank introduces as 'very important people', arrive. The woman asks Alex about his treatment. Alex reveals that when he now hears Beethoven's *Ninth Symphony*, he just wants to die. Soon afterwards he collapses. The next scene (35, 117:59) starts with a close-up of Alex being woken up in a top-floor bedroom by Beethoven's *Ninth*, already very sick. Frank and the others wait in a room below, Frank grinning ecstatically. Alex is in pain and eventually jumps out of the window. We next (Scene 36, 121:00) see him covered in plaster and moaning. A nurse and a doctor who are having sex behind a curtain eventually realise that he has recovered consciousness. This is followed (Scene 37, 122:09) by a montage of newspaper frontpages, blaming the government for Alex's suicide attempt. Next (Scene 38, 122:38), we see Alex's parents at his bed; his mother is crying, while his father offers reconciliation. In the following scene (39, 123:54), a woman pushes a tray to Alex's bed. She introduces herself as Dr Taylor; she is a psychiatrist who wants to show him some slides. Alex is supposed to say what he imagines one of the people in the pictures to say. Alex provides violent as well as comic dialogue. In the next scene (40, 127:28), Alex is being fed at night when the Minister of the Interior arrives. While talking to Alex, he eventually takes over his feeding. He apologises to him, and offers Alex 'an interesting job at a salary which you would regard as adequate', in return for 'helping us' with the press. He then announces 'a little surprise'. A stereo system with huge loudspeakers is pushed into the room, playing Beethoven's *Ninth Symphony*. Photographers gather in front of Alex's bed to take pictures of him being held by the minister. The film cuts from a close-up of Alex's face to a shot of a naked couple having sex in the snow, surrounded by an audience of clapping aristocratic types. Alex's voiceover concludes: 'I was cured all right.' The credits begin (133:46), accompanied by Gene Kelly's version of 'Singin' in the Rain', which plays until the credits end (136:26).

 **PART 1**

KEY THEMES AND IDEAS

Introduction

In an interview with the *Chicago Tribune* in February 1972, less than two months after *A Clockwork Orange* had been released in the US, Stanley Kubrick was remarkably explicit about his intentions for the film and about the 'moral of the story':

> It's a satire, which is to say that you hold up current vices and folly to ridicule. You pretend to say the opposite of the truth in order to destroy it. The only exception to this is the chaplain ... . He states the moral of the story even though he is trotted out looking a bit of the buffoon. The essential moral of the story hinges on the question of choice, and the question of whether man can be good without having the choice to be evil, and whether a creature who no longer has this choice can still be a man. (Siskel, 1972/2001, p. 122)

Rather than just raising this question, Kubrick also offered an answer when he stated that, while 'Alex is the very personification of evil', the conditioning he receives constitutes 'a much greater evil' (pp. 122–3). With reference to the current political climate and to public anxieties 'in a city like New York where people feel very unsafe', he also suggested that 'people eventually become very disturbed ..., leaning toward more authority of a much tougher kind'; 'the danger is not that authority will collapse, but that, finally, in order to preserve itself, it ... will become very repressive' (p. 119). This statement aligns Kubrick with the political sentiments expressed by Frank Alexander in Scene 33. He may be overly agitated, thus 'looking a bit of the buffoon', much like the chaplain, but what he says can still be taken seriously:

> The government's big boast … is the way they have dealt with crime during the past few months. Recruiting brutal young toughs into the police, proposing debilitating and will-sapping techniques of conditioning. Oh, we've seen it all before in other countries. The thin end of the wedge. Before we know where we are we shall have the full apparatus of totalitarianism.

Based on the above interview statements and on the film's dialogue, it is tempting, then, to approach *A Clockwork Orange* as an exercise in moral philosophy or a moral and political critique of the totalitarian tendencies of contemporary governments, indeed of the modern state.[9] However, as noted at the end of the Introduction, in an earlier interview Kubrick had explicitly denied that *A Clockwork Orange* was 'primarily or even significantly, a topical, social story', describing it instead as an exploration of the subconscious and of human nature (Hofsess, 1971/2001, pp. 106–7), themes he also mentioned in passing when talking to the *Chicago Tribune* about recognising 'our own unconscious' in Alex and about 'man's capacity for violence' being 'an evolutionary hangover' (Siskel, 1972/2001, p. 123). So, as far as Kubrick was concerned, the film was obviously meant to operate at several, very different levels. In this part, I explore some of these levels, first of all by briefly situating *A Clockwork Orange* in the context of Kubrick's films up to this point and by discussing the relationship between violence, human nature and politics. Here I will draw on Kubrick's comments about the film and relate them to what actually happens in it, paying particular attention to statements made by film characters that support or contradict the filmmaker. Second, I go on to analyse the relationship between art, violence and life, both in the film and in Kubrick's comments on it. Finally, I outline the explanations provided by Kubrick and by Anthony Burgess for the film's title, before moving on to discuss a much broader range of meanings than Burgess and Kubrick allowed for in their statements, and how these meanings of the title could be seen to play out across the film.

Violence, Human Nature and Politics

For someone who later came to be perceived as an uncommunicative recluse (cp. Simpson, 2008), Kubrick was surprisingly eager to talk to the press about *A Clockwork Orange*. In fact, far from being habitually withdrawn, Kubrick had courted journalists and been involved in the marketing of his films ever since he began making them in the early 1950s (Krämer, forthcoming b). In his many interviews about *A Clockwork Orange*, most of them given in conjunction with the film's release in 1971 and 1972, Kubrick was frequently asked to debate the topic of violence. This was partly due to the fact that violence – both of the interpersonal and of the institutional variety – was so central not only to this film but also to almost all of his earlier work, beginning with his debut, the short boxing documentary, *Day of the Fight* (1951). Kubrick's feature films had dealt with military organisations and combat (*Fear and Desire*, 1953; *Paths of Glory*, 1957; *Spartacus*, 1960; *Dr. Strangelove or: How I Learned to Stop Worrying and Love the Bomb*, 1964) or with criminal violence (*Killer's Kiss*, 1955; *The Killing*, 1956; *Lolita*, 1962). The only previous feature of his that did not deal explicitly with the military or with crime was *2001: A Space Odyssey* (1968). However, this film traced the very origins of humanity to the prehistoric discovery by ape-like creatures of tools that could be used as murderous weapons. *2001* continued to play very successfully in movie theatres in the early 1970s (Lewin, 1972; Krämer, 2010b, p. 93) and thus was very much on the minds of both journalists and audiences – and indeed on Kubrick's mind – when *A Clockwork Orange* came out.

Drawing out the implications of the story he had told in *2001*, Kubrick – introduced by the *Daily Mail* as 'no stranger to violence', which is 'the common denominator in all his films' – discussed *A Clockwork Orange* with reference to his basic conception of human nature:

> Although a certain amount of hypocrisy exists about it …, everyone is fascinated by violence. … After all, man is the most remorseless killer who ever stalked the earth. Our interest in violence in part reflects the

fact that on the subconscious level we are very little different from our primitive ancestors. (Cable, 1971)

In appealing to the viewers' unconscious, *A Clockwork Orange* addressed their most fundamental, most ancient, most 'primitive' level of being, and it did so by displaying Alex's 'primitive' violent behaviour in an attractive fashion:

Alex symbolizes man in his natural state, the way he would be if society did not impose its 'civilizing' processes upon him. What we respond to subconsciously is Alex's guiltless sense of freedom to kill and rape, and to be our savage natural selves. (Weinraub, 1972)

Because the film presents Alex in such a way as to enable him to draw 'the audience into his own vision of life', a brutal life from which he initially derives a lot of pleasure, viewers are, according to Kubrick, vicariously experiencing Alex's 'freedom', violence and lack of guilt as 'most enjoyable' (Weinraub, 1972).

Unlike Kubrick's statements cited in the introduction to this part which were mirrored in those made by the prison chaplain and by Frank Alexander in the film, with regards to the viewers' enjoyment, *A Clockwork Orange* offers a counterperspective to Kubrick's when Dr Branom tells Alex in Scene 26: 'when we are healthy, we respond to the presence of the hateful with fear and nausea'. As an effect of the Ludovico treatment Alex, who revelled in both real and filmic violence ('doing it or watching it, I used to feel real horrorshow'), is now sickened by the mere sight of it, which, Dr Branom argues, shows that he is 'becoming healthy'. However compromised Dr Branom may be, her statement does raise the question of whether it is 'healthy' to take pleasure in violent films, indeed whether it is healthy for viewers of *A Clockwork Orange* to enjoy themselves when watching it. In his interviews, Kubrick acknowledged this concern:

on the psychological dream content level, you can regard Alex as a creature of the id. He is within all of us. ... [S]ome people ... are unable to accept this view of themselves and, therefore, they become angry at the film. (Strick and Houston, 1972/2001, p. 129)

Kubrick implied that it was perfectly natural to indulge in 'primitive' fantasies (after all, this happened nightly in people's dreams), and also that conscious reflection on the unconscious workings of one's mind led people to realise 'uncomfortable' and aggravating truths about themselves. This realisation went hand in hand with the suspension of their fascination with, and their vicarious involvement in, Alex's worldview and behaviour. Despite his emphasis on people's 'savage nature', Kubrick seemed to assume – not unlike Dr Branom – that on some level they were deeply averse to violence. Indeed, according to Kubrick, when first encountering Alex, the audience's fascination is mixed with aversion; it is only when Alex seduces the audience, much like '[Shakespeare's] Richard III [who] gradually undermines your disapproval of his evil ways', that 'you find yourself drawn very quickly into [Alex's] world and find yourself seeing things through his eyes' (Weinraub, 1972; Houston, 1971/2001, p. 110). Thus, according to Kubrick, both at the very beginning of the audience's engagement with Alex and after it has ended, viewers do in fact reject 'his evil ways'.

What, then, is the purpose of confronting viewers with Alex and through him with their own savage nature? In Kubrick's view, this confrontation had a psychologically cathartic, an intellectually stimulating, and a satisfyingly artistic dimension. Most immediately, he argued, '[o]ur subconscious finds release in Alex, just as it finds release in dreams (Houston, 1971/2001, p. 110). Kubrick went further, partly in response to criticisms of the film, especially the anxieties about its possible negative impact on audiences:

There may be an argument in support of saying that any kind of violence in films, in fact, serves a useful social purpose by allowing people a means of vicariously freeing themselves from the pent-up, aggressive emotions which are better expressed in dreams, or in the dreamlike state of watching a film than in potentially harmful action (Strick and Houston, 1972/2001, p. 130). Very cautiously, Kubrick suggested that films like *A Clockwork Orange* might play a positive role in society, preventing violence rather than encouraging it. Interestingly, this is exactly the function that films fulfil within the story of *A Clockwork Orange*. However, here they only do so with the support of drugs that put the subject of the Ludovico treatment into an unbearable 'death-like paralysis' during which, as Dr Brodsky explains in Scene 25, he 'will make his most rewarding associations between his catastrophic experience-environment and the violence he sees', with the ultimate effect that in future he is going to be unable even to contemplate violent action, let alone to behave violently. Thus, Kubrick's interview statements about film violence facilitating catharsis contrast sharply with *A Clockwork Orange*'s story about film violence helping to produce an insurmountable aversion to violence in the viewer – but, as I mentioned earlier, Kubrick expected such aversion to be part of the audience's psychological make-up anyway, so that viewers would automatically reject their initial, positive response to film violence once they became aware of it.

In addition to the psychological function of his film, Kubrick, as we have already seen, expected it to play a role in debates about morality (which is the 'greater evil': Alex's criminal behaviour or the state's suppression of it through psychological conditioning?) and politics (what is the likely outcome of pervasive challenges to the state's authority: anarchy or totalitarianism?). There is a tension between the idea that the film's contribution to such debates was to pose questions which forced viewers to make up their own minds, and the suggestion that the film itself presented answers. In interviews, Kubrick certainly articulated his own answers to the questions the film posed (psychological conditioning is the 'greater evil'; totalitarianism is a more likely outcome than anarchy), but he also suggested that viewers had to make up their own minds in response to the film. For example, he emphasised that viewers had to be confronted with a strong moral dilemma:

> If Alex were a lesser villain, … [i]t would … be like one of those westerns where they purport to be doing a film which is against lynching and so

they lynch innocent people. The point of the film seems to be: You shouldn't lynch people because you might lynch innocent people; rather than: You shouldn't lynch anybody. Obviously, if Alex were a lesser villain, it would be very easy to reject his treatment. (Siskel, 1972/2001, p. 123)

This is a rather defensive and unconvincing statement. The film *does* make it easy to reject the Ludovico treatment because in many ways Alex is presented, as Kubrick freely admits, as an attractive character, especially when compared to just about everyone else in the film; Kubrick notes 'his candor and wit and intelligence, and the fact that all the other characters are lesser people, and in some ways worse people' (Houston, 1971/2007, p. 110). In addition, this appealing protagonist is shown to suffer greatly – and the audience is invited to suffer with him – both during the Ludovico treatment and afterwards. Interestingly, Alex's suffering is precisely the angle that Frank Alexander and his political allies want to highlight in their campaign against the Ludovico treatment in particular and the government in general. Alexander describes Alex in Scenes 32 and 33 as 'the poor victim of this horrible new technique', 'tortured in prison, then thrown out to be tortured by the police', 'a living witness' to the government's 'diabolical' policies. Indeed, as the newspaper headlines shown in Scene 37 demonstrate, this emotional rhetoric is highly contagious and effective, forcing the Minister of the Interior to reverse his policies. Both within the film's story and, I would think, in our response to the film, it is made all too easy to resolve the moral dilemma it poses.

In any case, asking – as Kubrick said the film did – whether it is better that Alex is violent and free or that he is non-violent and conditioned does not seem very productive, because, obviously, there are many possible gradations of freedom and of violence, which do not lend themselves to an either/or choice. Even after the Ludovico treatment, Alex's choices are only restricted in certain, very limited, albeit for him extremely important, areas. He can still choose to listen to all music except for Beethoven's *Ninth Symphony* and he can fall in love (but not have sex); he could even use his charm and wit, his verbal and social dexterity to embark on a different kind of criminal career which avoids violence, but might include other ways of dominating, humiliating and hurting people. So, the film's moral dilemma is based on a rather false dichotomy. Similarly, Kubrick's reflections in interviews on the likelihood of anarchy or totalitarianism do not altogether tally with what happens in the film: after all, in it the government quickly reverses its policy because, as the Minister of the Interior says in Scene 40, in the face of hostile press reports and changes in public opinion, it 'has lost a lot of popularity' and might be voted out 'at the next election'. Obviously the minister hopes to mobilise Alex in a public-relations offensive aimed at 'changing the public's verdict' so as to be able to win the election, but this would appear to be business as usual in a democracy. If the government was in fact totalitarian, would it be so sensitive to the press and to public opinion, so eager to improve its image? Hence, Kubrick's comments on the film once again do not do justice to the complexities of the story it tells.

There is perhaps a good reason for this mismatch. It seems that, in response to the quickly escalating controversy, Kubrick felt compelled, in particular with regards to the film's seductive portrayal of Alex, to be more explicit and one-sided, indeed simplistic about his personal views and what the message of the film might be than was appropriate and than he was comfortable with. Indeed, in some of his earliest interviews about *A Clockwork Orange*, Kubrick refused to go into too much detail in order to ensure that viewers' responses were not unduly influenced by him. One interviewer noted: 'Kubrick is reluctant to discuss the meaning of *A Clockwork Orange*', because the film was not meant to present a particular 'doctrine or … political philosophy …, but most important because he thinks any direct discussion of the film can only diminish it' (Cable, 1971; cp. Zimmerman, 1972, p. 33). Kubrick certainly thought that the controversy surrounding the film, insofar as it focused on the question of whether violent films could cause violent behaviour, diminished its potential intellectual impact. This question suggested a simplistic answer to the all-important issue of how one might explain such behaviour. The issue is stated explicitly in the film by Mr Deltoid in Scene 10:

> What gets into you all? … We have been studying [the problem] for damn well near a century, yes, but we get no further with our studies. You've got a good home here, good loving parents, you've got not too bad of a brain.

Unable to come up with an answer, Deltoid, probably jokingly, evokes supernatural forces: 'Is it some devil that crawls inside of you?' The film as a whole does not reveal any obvious reason for Alex's extremely aggressive behaviour – although it hints at all sorts of social factors which could be said to help prepare the ground for it (ranging from his clueless and ineffectual parents and the run-down and ugly block of flats in which he lives to his peer culture, the free availability of drugs and police brutality).

Having dedicated most of his career to exploring human violence, Kubrick obviously took its explanation very seriously, and regretted that *A Clockwork Orange*, instead of being seen to address this issue in a new way, got caught up in the debate about media effects:

> To focus one's interest on this aspect of violence is to ignore the principal causes, which I would list as:
> 1. Original sin: the religious view.
> 2. Unjust economic exploitation: the Marxist view.
> 3. Emotional and psychological frustration: the psychological view.
> 4. Genetic factors based on the 'Y' chromosome theory: the biological view.
> 5. Man – the killer ape: the evolutionary view. (Kubrick, quoted in Strick and Houston, 1972/2001, p. 129)

Kubrick insisted on the necessity of such a multilayered discussion of violence, combining the consideration of fundamental human characteristics (elsewhere referred to as 'human nature') with the analysis of particular socioeconomic and political contexts as well as specific situational and individual factors. In very general terms, he made the point that 'moral and political philosophy' and the design of political systems and institutions as well as of particular policies needed to be based on an adequate understanding of fundamental human characteristics, including a certain propensity for violence: 'One of the most dangerous fallacies … is that man is essentially good, and that it is society which makes him bad' (Weinraub, 1972). More specifically, he was dismayed by the unproductive and indeed harmful diversion of policy debates into claims about media effects: 'By directing a lot of media attention to whether films and television contribute to violence, politicians conveniently escape looking at the real causes of violence in society' (Siskel, 1972/2001, p. 125). Now, within the film, the government, avoiding both the fallacy that 'man is essentially good' and a distracting debate about media effects, is arguably addressing some of these 'real causes' head on, namely the basic human capacity for violence and the particularly strong criminal inclinations – much enhanced by the time they may spend in prison, as the minister points out in Scenes 22 and 28 – of individuals such as Alex. Kubrick would appear to object to that government's methods but applaud its willingness to address the problem and to do so with a healthy scepticism about human goodness.

So far I have explored how watching *A Clockwork Orange* and thus being confronted with their own 'savage natures' was meant to be psychologically cathartic and intellectually stimulating for the film's viewers. Despite the obvious importance of these two goals, however, Kubrick made it very clear that, more than anything else, *A Clockwork Orange* was designed to please its audience as a work of art.

Art, Violence and Life

In interviews, Kubrick insisted that he did not select his film projects – most of which were based on novels – on the basis of a specific thematic concern: 'I don't start by saying, "What am I concerned about, and where can I find a story that relates to that?"' (Siskel, 1972/2001, p. 118). Instead he looked for what one might call formal or aesthetic qualities. With regards to Burgess's *A Clockwork Orange*, he said: 'What attracted me to the book was its qualities as a work of art' (Siskel, 1972/2001, p. 118). In addition to the novel's 'brilliantly developed' ideas, Kubrick praised its 'narrative invention', its 'bizarre and exciting characters' and its language (Houston, 1971/2001, p. 109). In particular, Kubrick liked 'the symmetry of its plot wherein each of Alex's victims appears again in the final section to deliver retribution'; for Kubrick this symmetry did not primarily serve to deliver a moral lesson (along the lines of 'what goes around, comes around'), but was an attractive formal quality in its own right (Houston, 1971/2001, p. 111). With regards to filmmaking, he stated: 'in addition to any higher purpose you may have in mind, you must be interesting; visually interesting, narratively interesting, interesting from an acting point of view' (Strick and Houston, 1972/2001, p. 131). Without Kubrick making this explicit, we can easily see that once again symmetry (of visual composition as well as narrative construction) plays an important role in his aesthetic concerns, although such symmetry is never perfect, always slightly off balance (figs. 3–5, showing Mr Deltoid, the Catlady and the prison yard). Being interesting in this way allowed a film to achieve the primary function of the 'work of art' which, in Kubrick's view, was to be 'always exhilarating and never depressing, whatever its subject matter may be', and through this to 'make life more enjoyable or more endurable' (p. 130).

Importantly, the story of *A Clockwork Orange* foregrounds the exhilaration produced by art through Alex's enjoyment of music, notably Beethoven's *Ninth Symphony*. When he hears the woman singing the 'Ode to Joy' in Scene 6, his pleasure is expressed through his facial expression and his voiceover: 'I felt all the malenky [tiny] little hairs on my plott [body] standing endwise and the shivers crawling up like slow malenky lizards and then down again.' It is precisely the disruption of this pleasure by Dim's rude noise that sets in motion a series of events which leads to Alex's downfall: Alex hits Dim who then gangs up with Georgie the next day (Scene 13), eventually taking revenge by smashing a milk bottle in Alex's face and leaving him to be arrested

3

4

5

by the police (Scene 16). Appreciation of art, or lack of such appreciation, also plays a role in the run-up to Alex's killing of the Catlady. In Scene 16 he is intrigued by the penis sculpture and starts to play with it, which upsets its owner: 'Don't touch it. It's a very important work of art.' This in turn encourages Alex to provoke her further by hitting the sculpture, which angers the woman so much that she attacks him with a Beethoven bust; this eventually leads Alex to smash the sculpture into her head and kill her. In the same scene Alex also comments on the nude paintings, with their graphic displays of female genitalia, hanging on the wall: 'Naughty, naughty, naughty. You filthy old soomka.' He is suggesting that the woman is deriving sensual, even sexual pleasure from her art. With this statement, Alex appears to project his own response to music onto the woman. When he previously listened to the *Ninth Symphony* in his room (Scene 8), his face expressed intense, perhaps orgiastic (and masturbatory) pleasure. At the same time, his voiceover described an uplifting experience bordering on the spiritual: 'Oh, bliss, bliss and heaven … . It was like a bird of rarest spun heaven metal, or like silvery wine flowing in a space ship, gravity all nonsense now.'

When, after his imprisonment for manslaughter and his volunteering for the Ludovico treatment, Alex encounters the *Ninth Symphony* again in Scene 27, it becomes associated with intense suffering. The music accompanies the films he is shown during his treatment, which, in conjunction with the drugs he has been given, cause him, in Dr Brodsky's words (from Scene 25), 'to experience … deep feelings of terror and helplessness … a sense of stifling or drowning'. This shocking conversion of his previous ecstasy into terror, of his uplift into drowning, makes Alex scream in protest: 'It's not fair I should feel ill when I hear lovely, lovely Ludwig van.' Dr Brodsky comments: 'Here's the punishment element perhaps.' Indeed, when Alex talks to Frank Alexander's associates in Scene 34, they are mainly interested in his inadvertent conditioning against the *Ninth Symphony*. Initially we might think that this is because they want to exploit this angle in their political campaigning, but then it is revealed that they are looking for a sure way to drive Alex to suicide. He tells them that, when he now hears this music, 'all I can think about is like trying to snuff it', that is to die, which is exactly what he tries to do by jumping out of the window in the next scene. From Frank Alexander's facial expression we know that he considers this to be just punishment for his tormentor and also an immensely satisfying act of revenge. In this way, the film foregrounds not only Alex's enjoyment of music, but also the terrible consequences any disruption of this enjoyment (first through Dim and then through the Ludovico treatment) has for him. This puts enormous weight on the ending of the final scene, in which it is revealed that Alex's enjoyment of the *Ninth Symphony* has been restored. The return of his ecstatic facial expression, together with the scene he fantasises and his voiceover ('I was cured all right'), highlights the fact that the effect of music is central to Alex's existence, 'always exhilarating and never depressing', to quote Kubrick's comments on art, and serving 'to make life more enjoyable'.

There is a tension between Kubrick's demand that a work of art should and can have a life-enhancing impact 'whatever its subject matter may be', and the images that Alex projects onto the music he enjoys: dancing Jesuses (naked and with visible wounds), a hanging, explosions, rocks falling on people, a volcano erupting, Alex as a vampire (all of these in Scene 8), a couple having sex in public (in Scene 40). For Alex, blasphemy, violence and sex become the 'subject matter' of Beethoven's *Ninth Symphony*, which might make us reluctant to apply Kubrick's claim that what is important about art is its 'exhilarating' impact rather than its content to Alex's response to the *Ninth Symphony*. Our reluctance is surely strengthened by the fact that elsewhere music is not simply associated with Alex's mental images but with his behaviour. In Scene 5 he kicks Frank Alexander and prepares to rape his wife while singing 'Singin' in the Rain', the lyrics of which are directly applicable to his actions: 'What a glorious feeling / I'm happy again / ... / I'm ready for love' (with Dim repeating 'ready for love' several times). In Scene 14, he is contemplating Georgie and Dim's challenge to his authority when 'it was lovely music that came to my aid'; hearing Rossini's *The Thieving Magpie* through a nearby window, he embarks on a vicious attack on the two rebellious droogs. Furthermore, in Scene 11, he lures two girls to his room by promising both sex and music: 'Come with uncle and hear all proper. Hear angel trumpets and devil trombones.' The following scene shows him having sex accompanied by music. In this way, a close link is established between Alex's enjoyment of music, the fantasies of sex and violence he associates with it, and his sexual and violent behaviour. What is more, the pervasiveness of mostly very graphic and sexually explicit representations of women (most notably, the furniture of the Korova Milk Bar and the Catlady's paintings) suggests a connection between a cultural atmosphere characterised by the objectification of women and Alex's sexual fantasies as well as his sexual assault on Mrs Alexander. In this way, the film hints at links between the 'subject matter' of 'art' and violent as well as sexual behaviour. At the same time, it also seems to celebrate the 'pure' enjoyment of music (and art in general), irrespective of whatever content one might project onto it.

The tension between a conception of art that defines it as ultimately contentless and purely formal, and a different view which highlights the artwork's connections to social reality (through its content and its possible impact on its audience) is foregrounded in Kubrick's discussion, and the film's representation, of dance. Kubrick explained that the film's 'stylised' violence resulted from his wish to find an equivalent of the novel's innovative 'writing style':

> The first section of the film that incorporates most of the violent action is principally organized around the Overture to Rossini's *Thieving Magpie*, and, in a very broad sense, you could say that the violence is turned into dance. (Houston, 1971/2001, p. 111)

Of course, in the film's story, it is Alex who turns his brutal attack on Mr and Mrs Alexander into a little dance when he moves and kicks and slaps his victims to the rhythm of 'Singin' in the Rain'. Indeed, it appears that the whole scene is orchestrated – or directed – by Alex.He gives instructions to his droogs, redesigns the set by throwing things around and smashing up furniture, and then hums and sings his own soundtrack. In other words, Alex creates a theatrical scene, a work of art. One might say that this severely compromises Kubrick's stance on the disconnectedness and self-referentiality of art, because Alex's 'art' is here shown to hurt people – indeed, that is its main purpose. Furthermore, when, in Scenes 25 and 27, Alex is shown films during the Ludovico treatment, sitting in front of a big screen (much like the audience of *A Clockwork Orange*) and unable to avert his eyes (much like those members of the audience who find the images so compelling that they cannot look away even – and especially – when these images contain extreme violence), he is clearly suffering tremendously. So the story depends on our willingness to accept the premise that (with a little help from unspecified medication), watching films can be unbearably painful. Once again, this constitutes a challenge to Kubrick's interview statements about art. In fact, the film's credit sequence, which is accompanied by Gene Kelly's version of 'Singin' in the Rain', reiterates that challenge. On the one hand, we might say that just when they are about to leave the cinema, viewers are reminded that for them the song is forever tainted by its association with the film *A Clockwork Orange*, much like Beethoven's *Ninth Symphony* was ruined for Alex during the Ludovico treatment. On the other hand, the memory of what Alex did when first humming and singing the song does, on some level, raise the question for the audience of what it would be like to act out this song in the same way; alternatively, a viewer might wonder whether other audience members (especially young males) contemplated such acting out.

In other words, both narratively and stylistically the film seems to be designed in such a way that the audience is constantly reminded of the intimate, and potentially highly destructive, relationship between art and life. In interviews, however, Kubrick only acknowledged that art could bring joy to the audience and lift its spirits, pretty much denying any further connection: 'I don't think that any work of art has a responsibility to be anything but a work of art' (Strick and Houston, 1972/2001, p. 130). Responding once again to the attacks on the film, he insisted that art certainly could not change people:

> It has been demonstrated that even after deep hypnosis, in the post-hypnotic state, people will not do what is contrary to their nature, so that the idea that people can be corrupted by a film is, I think, completely wrong. (Siskel, 1972/2001, p. 124)

Art could only ever be affirmative – in the most general sense affirmative of life and, more specifically, affirmative of what the audience already brought to it: '[Works of art] affect us when they illuminate something we already feel, they don't change us' (McGregor, 1972, p. 13). Kubrick went as far as to make the following astonishing claim: 'I certainly wouldn't have said my life has been influenced by any work of art' (p. 13).

Once again, I think that such categorical statements can be explained by the filmmaker's wish to defend his film, and himself, against accusations of exerting a harmful influence on cinemagoers. At the same time, there is, in my view, also a genuine modesty, even humility at work here, a recognition by the filmmaker of the limits of the (positive or negative) role that films, or other works of art, can play in people's lives, an (implicit) acknowledgement that for most, if not all, people, family, health, politics and suchlike are much more important than cinemagoing, visits to the museum, listening to music etc. In any case, Kubrick's comments on the doubly affirmative role of art do give it a certain importance, and, as we saw earlier, his insistence that the only 'responsibility' a work of art has is 'to be … a work of art' does not at all preclude that it also develops themes, expresses ideas, stimulates reflection and contributes to discussion. So let's take another look at what these themes and ideas might be, using the film's title as a starting point.

What Is a 'Clockwork Orange'?

Explanations of the film's title were available to its viewers. The press book for *A Clockwork Orange* contained what was described as Anthony Burgess's 'ultimate clarification' of the title, which was in turn referenced in many articles about the film:

> In 1945, back from the army, I heard an 80-year-old cockney in a London pub say that somebody was 'as queer as a clockwork orange'. The 'queer' did not mean homosexual; it meant mad. … [Man] is a growth as organic as a fruit, capable of color, fragrance and sweetness; to meddle with him, condition him, is to turn him into a mechanical creation. (Warner Bros., 1972, p. 2)

Kubrick explained in one of his interviews: 'It is necessary for man to have the choice to be good or evil, even if he chooses evil. To deprive him of this choice is to make him something less than human – a clockwork orange' (Houston, 1972/2001, p. 128). He also said that the film dealt with the 'immorality' of depriving 'a man of his freedom, by imprisoning him, or of his free will, by turning him into a clockwork orange, a robot being' (Gelmis, 1972). These references to, and explanations of, the phrase 'a clockwork orange' show that it is intimately linked to the film's themes and ideas as I have discussed them so far.[10] However, there is more to the potential meanings of this phrase than the above quotations suggest.

To begin with, it is important to note that – unlike the novel – the film does not contain any explicit explanation of its title, thus encouraging those viewers who did not read about it, and even those who did, to make up their own minds about what 'clockwork orange' might mean. The phrase evokes the image of the inner workings of a clock placed inside an orange, and, more abstractly, it suggests that an organic thing (a fruit) can contain, and perhaps be controlled by, an artificial mechanism (a clockwork). Most generally, it could be said to express the idea that living and non-living matter, organisms and technologies can be intimately intertwined. One might even go as far as associating 'clockwork' with ticking, which would turn the orange into a kind of timebomb, or, alternatively, give it an artificial heart beating in its interior. There is also the possibility to project the phrase 'runs like clockwork' onto the orange; taken literally rather than metaphorically, this conjures up the image of a usually inanimate object starting to move or to interact in some other way with the world around it.

When viewing the film, the audience is invited to apply the many potential meanings of this phrase to something or someone in the story. An initial candidate is the assemblage of lifelike sculptures of naked women used as furniture in the Korova Milk Bar. In Scene 6, their lifelikeness is foregrounded, when Dim addresses one of the sculptures, which functions as a milk dispenser, as 'Lucy' while filling his glass with the milk coming out of one of her nipples (fig. 6). Relatedly, in Scene 16 Alex brings the sculpture of the giant phallus to life by hitting it so that it begins to jiggle back and forth, not unlike an obscene metronome. More generally, several scenes up to this point focus on objects that are given lifelike qualities mainly by foregrounding their sexual dimension. The murals in the lobby of Alex's block of flats feature naked men, who have been given speech bubbles and erections (Scenes 7 and 13). In Alex's room a snake crawls between the widely spread legs of a naked woman in a painting, as if to enter her vagina (Scene 8). A rapidly edited

6

sequence, cut to the rhythm of Beethoven's *Ninth Symphony*, appears to transform four small Jesus sculptures into a mini *corps de ballet*, merrily dancing away. The phallic icecream cones licked by the two young women Alex approaches in the record shop (Scene 12) provoke him to comment: 'Enjoying that, are you my darling? Bit cold and pointless, isn't it, my lovely?' Finally, the mansion in Scene 16 is full of extremely graphic paintings of naked women. Thus, the film's first third foregrounds the lifelikeness and sexuality of paintings and three-dimensional objects.

It also emphasises the mechanical qualities and artificial appendages of the human body. There are Alex's false eyelashes in the very first shot of the story, later to be removed from his face in Scene 8. The droogs' genitalia are both hidden behind and foregrounded through their massive cod-pieces, which they wear above their trousers (Scenes 1–7, 13–16); in several shots, the droogs seem to let it all hang out, when in fact what we see is only plastic (fig. 7). When Alex cuts away bits of clothing of the woman he is about to rape in Scene 5, the fact that she is gagged and held tightly by Dim takes away much of her humanity, making her appear in several long shots more like a

7

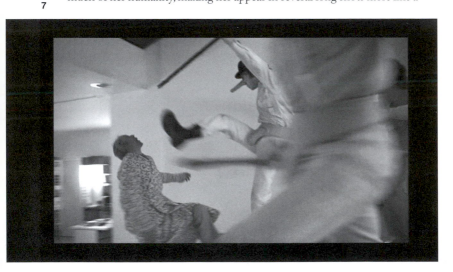

mannequin than a human being. When Alex has sex with the two young women in Scene 12, their movements are speeded up so much that they appear no longer human; instead their intertwining bodies move like a mechanism in overdrive. The film makes this sense of objectification of the human body explicit when Alex rams the sculpture into the woman's face in Scene 16; at the very moment when we expect the sculpture to make contact with her head, it is replaced by shots of paintings of mouths, breasts and a vagina (the latter covered by a woman's hand). More generally, as noted earlier, much of the action in the first third of the film has people moving to the rhythm of music, as if the music controlled them. This is the case in the curious dance that unfolds on the stage in Scene 3, involving Billyboy's gang and their victim, and the balletic fight that then ensues between them and Alex's gang. It also applies to Alex's attack on the Alexanders in Scene 5, carried out to the rhythm of 'Singin' in the Rain'. Similarly, the orgy in Scene 12 is in synch with the music's frantic rhythm. When Alex attacks Dim and Georgie in Scene 14, it is shown in slow motion, their movements once again synchronised with the music. While there is less of a sense of control through music in Scene 16, Alex's fight with the Catlady is nevertheless much like a dance.

Up to this point, then, the film shows Alex subjecting himself willingly to musical rhythms, and making others part of his violent dances, while people often appear (to him and to the camera) like objects, as, in turn, objects and paintings come alive, especially through graphic sexual imagery, thus tracing out some of the possible meanings of the phrase 'clockwork orange'. Subsequent scenes can be understood as bringing out the phrase's meanings in a very different manner. Now, Alex's movements as well as, later on, his mental states, are controlled by others. In Scene 17, he is trapped in a bare room and eventually driven into a corner. Indeed, from then on, he is moving much less than in the film's first third. He is mostly sitting still during the prison chaplain's sermon (Scene 19) and in the prison library (Scene 20), spends most of his time in the Ludovico facility lying in bed (Scenes 24 and 26) or tied down to a chair in its film theatre (Scenes 25 and 27). During his second visit to Frank Alexander's house, we see him lying in a bathtub and sitting on a chair (Scenes 33 and 34). During his time in hospital, he is almost completely immobilised by the plaster that covers much of his body (Scenes 36, 38–40). Whenever Alex has some mobility, his movements are, directly or indirectly, controlled by others. When he arrives at the prison in Scene 18, he is subjected to a rigorous routine; his position is determined by lines on the floor and by the furniture, his movements follow the instructions of the chief guard. Lines on the floor and precise commands from the chief guard also determine Alex's position and actions when he is in the prison courtyard (Scene 21) and when he sees the prison governor (Scene 22). In addition, guards control Alex's movements when he is delivered to the Ludovico facility (Scene 23). When he finally gets up from his chair in the prison library (Scene 20), he is guided by the chaplain, and then stands still. The drunk he encounters again in Scene 30 pulls him along to a nearby underpass, from where Dim and Georgie drag him away, first to their police car and then to a trough in the woods (Scene 31). Upon arriving at Mr Alexander's house, he is so exhausted that he needs to be carried around (Scene 32). Ironically, the only place where he would like to stay still and linger – his parents' flat and within it his old room – he is in effect barred from (Scene 29).

In addition to being physically immobilised (motionless like an orange would be) or having his movements controlled by others (as if a clockwork mechanism was responsible for them), Alex's inner being is subjected to ever higher levels of control as well (as if the clockwork not only determined his exterior, physical actions but also his interior, mental activity). In Scenes 25 and 27, the combination of drugs and films creates sickening sensations, as do the carefully staged violent and sexual provocations in Scene 28. In Scene 35, he is once again trapped in a room, and music is used to replicate his previous torture during the Ludovico treatment, only now he is given enough mobility so as to be able to try to put an end to his suffering. In all of these scenes, every aspect of Alex's being is controlled by others, his ability to move, his physical sensations, his mental anguish; even his attempts to alleviate his suffering can be calculated in advance so that they unfold like a programme, like clockwork.

This is indeed a dramatic reversal from the first third of the film when Alex was mainly in control of his own movements and those of others, when he used music to stimulate himself and to co-ordinate the action. And where previously Alex treated other people like objects – with the film replicating his objectifying view of them – once he is arrested by the police, he is not only physically abused but has more and more aspects of his humanity taken away from him. He loses his name and is given a number in prison (Scenes 18–23). Although he recovers his name in the Ludovico facility, he now becomes a test subject (both Dr Brodsky and the minister refer to him as 'the subject' in Scenes 25 and 28), a guinea pig for a laboratory experiment, no longer a person. This is also emphasised by the straitjacket he wears in the cinema, and by the way he is tied down to a chair and his eyes are kept open by a contraption on his head; his body largely disappears from view, apparently merging with the chair on which he sits, and only his face is alive (fig. 8). Similarly, when he wakes up in the hospital (Scene 36), almost all of his body is covered in plaster (fig. 9). Until the end of the story, Alex remains partly hidden under, and immobilised by, plaster; once again, only his face is fully

8

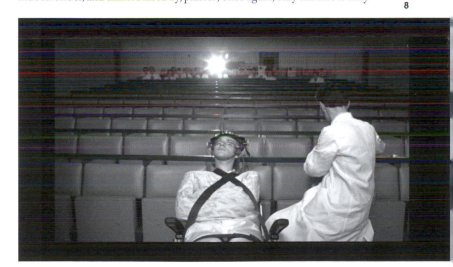

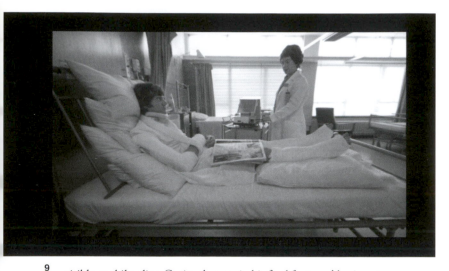

9

visible, mobile, alive. Curiously, even in his final fantasy, Alex is not very mobile, but is pinned down by the woman on top of him.

There are many different ways, then, in which the last two-thirds of the film show that Alex loses crucial aspects of his humanity, being conceived of and treated by others as an object rather than a person, having his ability to move reduced, with both his remaining mobility and his mental activity controlled by others, being physically merged with, and subdued by, non-living matter both in the cinema and in the hospital. At the very end of the story, Alex recovers his ability to enjoy the *Ninth Symphony* and sexual fantasies, and there is a promise from the Minister of the Interior that Alex will also be able to recover his ability to act exactly as he wants, once he gets out of the hospital. The film leaves open what exactly Alex will want to do with his regained external and internal freedom, but knowing that, in addition to music and sex, Alex has also recovered the ability to contemplate violence (as demonstrated by the psychological test in Scene 39), we have every reason to be apprehensive. While currently unable to do any harm, Alex might be ready for malevolent deeds in the near future; he is like a timebomb, a clockwork inside of him counting down the hours, minutes and seconds until he explodes into action. Indeed, looking back on the opening third of the film, we might want to consider the possibility that such a clockwork has always been driving him on. Where other people have a 'heart' and a conscience, Alex only seems to be motivated by the desire to gratify himself. Thus we could say that, long before he was subjected to the Ludovico treatment, an essential aspect of his humanity had been missing, pushed aside by a mechanism which converts impulse into action without consideration for the well-being of others. Alex has been a clockwork orange all along.

There remains one final twist in this exploration of how the film's title can be applied to *A Clockwork Orange*. Part of Alex's objectification takes place in a cinema, which reminds us of our own place in front of a screen. So, if the films Alex watches help to provoke calculated responses from him and to insert a sensual, emotional and behavioural programme into his brain, what might the film *A Clockwork Orange* be doing to us? Does the film turn us all into clockwork oranges? On a more positive note, we might also consider the fact that a film projector runs like clockwork so as to project twenty-four frames every single second, thus creating the illusion of movement and indeed of life, a version of life which can be more vivid and intense than our experiences outside the cinema. As Alex says in Scene 25: 'It's funny how the colours of the real world only seem really real when you viddy [see] them on the screen.' What is more, while a film like *A Clockwork Orange* appears to convey a series of events apparently evolving organically out of each other, both narratively and stylistically, it is in fact a meticulously constructed artefact, like a clockwork mechanism. Thus, we should not forget that the phrase 'clockwork orange' works both ways: it evokes the dangers of people being reduced to objects (oranges having clockworks inserted into them), but also the promise of objects coming to life (an orange animated by a clockwork mechanism). Whereas this promise is in line with Kubrick's insistence on the life-affirming power of art, the most heated attacks on *A Clockwork Orange* concerned the dangers of objectification, whereby the film was feared to do something to its viewers, who might then go on to objectify others.

Conclusion

In this part I have explored some of the main themes of *A Clockwork Orange* – in particular the relationship between violence, human nature, politics and art – with detailed reference to statements Stanley Kubrick made about the film. I have in turn tested some of these against what actually occurs in the film. Whether considering the film or Kubrick's interview statements, I have identified a number of ideas and suggestions which, quite understandably, might alarm critical observers: people are fundamentally 'savage' and 'primitive'; Alex acts that way and remains an attractive character; 'subconsciously', the audience enjoys his 'guiltless sense of freedom to kill and rape'; works of art (such as Beethoven's *Ninth Symphony*) can stimulate the violent fantasies and inspire the violent behaviour of young criminals such as Alex; as demonstrated by the Ludovico treatment, films can exert a powerful influence over their viewers, completely reshaping their outlook on life and their future behaviour; yet filmmakers (such as Stanley Kubrick) do not have to take responsibility for anything else but for creating art. These themes and ideas mirrored the worst fears of, and provided plenty of ammunition for, those people already worried about – and willing to take a stand against – the negative effects of modern media on their audiences. Of course, both Kubrick's statements and the film itself also offered a much more positive and optimistic counterperspective on the power of cinema (and art in general), highlighting the life-affirming and life-enhancing role it plays, the intellectual stimulation it provides, the cathartic release it offers. But, as Kubrick insisted, by and large films (and also interviews) 'affect us when they illuminate something we already feel', and otherwise can leave us cold. To a certain extent, we can only find *in* them what we bring *to* them.

In Part 2, I take another look at *A Clockwork Orange*, this time paying more attention to structure and style, with particular reference to some of the film's key scenes.

✖ Part 2

KEY SCENE ANALYSIS

Introduction

One of the earliest reviews of *A Clockwork Orange*, appearing in the American film-industry trade paper *Variety* on 15 December 1971, started with the following summary: 'Dispute-generating Stanley Kubrick film. Brutal, brilliant political allegory. Not for weak stomachs' (Murphy, 1971). From the very beginning, then, critical writing about *A Clockwork Orange* addressed not only the film's potential for controversy and its thematic preoccupations, but also registered the strong visceral response it generated in viewers, whose 'weak stomachs' might be adversely affected by the film's depiction of 'brutal' acts. Consciously or not, the *Variety* reviewer thus took a pointer from the Ludovico treatment within the film, which, he writes, causes Alex to become 'physically and mentally nauseous' – much like *A Clockwork Orange* may cause nausea in its audience. As the reviewer's comments on the film's ending indicate, he judged this strong response to have a deeply and confusingly emotional as well as a purely physiological dimension. Hearing Gene Kelly's version of 'Singin' in the Rain' over the credits may have a 'lesser impact than the earlier usage' during the attack on Mr and Mrs Alexander, yet 'the effect is still the same: does one laugh, or cry, or both?' Overall, the film's technical brilliance, its 'outrageous vulgarity, stark brutality and ... sophisticated comedy' as well as the 'predominantly erotic' atmosphere of its opening third and the 'opaque argument' presented in the remainder of the story ensured, in the reviewer's estimation, 'a broad audience potential of diverse and contradictory attitudes, each of which can probably find perverse solace'. There was, then, perhaps something 'perverse' about enjoying this film.

The New York *Morning Telegraph*'s Leo Mishkin found the futuristic vision of *A Clockwork Orange* 'absolutely horrifying', warning his readers that the film presented 'such sex and such violence as you have seldom seen before in the movies' (Mishkin, 1971). Mishkin describes the attacks on the drunk, the Alexanders and the Catlady in some detail and concludes what is meant to be a positive review as follows: 'It's a shocking, stomach-turning, vomitous motion picture, but more awful than anything else, it may just possibly prove to be true.' For yet other reviewers, the film's scenes of sex and violence left such a strong impression that they could not seriously engage with its thematic concerns and judged its technical brilliance to constitute a 'misuse of talent', even an abuse: 'Because Kubrick is such an accomplished craftsman, this film is the grisly ultimate in what writer Tom Wolfe calls "pornoviolence"' (*Christian Science Monitor*, 1971). Ultimately, 'it seems to drown in its own obscene violence' and is 'so repellent its "X" rating seems not warning enough'. Among the film's earliest British critics, who – like the Americans – were largely very positive about the film, Anne Edwards stood out by highlighting her visceral response to the film's 'deliberate viciousness, sadism, rape, murder and torture', judging it to be 'more explicit and more violent' than other recent controversial releases:

> It shows, in more shocking detail, in more sickening close-up than anything ever seen before how a young man addicted to 'ultra-violence and rape' leads his gang on group-raping and beating-up expeditions just for the fun of it. (Edwards, 1972)

In addition to the disgust she herself experienced in response to the film's 'pulped faces' and 'human beings treated like carcasses in a butcher's shop', Edwards also worried about the film's impact on others:

> How can anyone who supports a film like this escape the charge that it is violence in itself that fascinates and obsesses them, that whatever was intended the message that comes over most clearly is that violence can be enjoyed for its own sake, that violence is a thrill which many are invited to share …?

Edwards was worried that those who liked the film would learn its lesson about the enjoyability of violence and that, consequently – much like Alex in the first third of the film – they might come to take pleasure in actual violent behaviour. Yet, she also foregrounded the negative physical response that the film's violence provoked in her and viewers like her, much like the Ludovico treatment did in the film's story. The film's supporters agreed with Edwards that such a negative response to the film's content was likely and that enjoyment of the film was somewhat 'perverse', yet they were less concerned about this perverse appreciation leading on to violent behaviour (certainly as far as they themselves were concerned), and indeed they implied that being able to stomach and enjoy *A Clockwork Orange* was perhaps an indication of their own superiority. Furthermore, where the film's detractors might see its technical brilliance as a problem, because it was in the service of enhancing the impact of violent scenes (both their nauseating effect on right-minded viewers and their seductive appeal to others), the film's supporters seemed to think that style could and should be appreciated in its own right, irrespective of content. Finally, both camps perceived certain problems with the overall structure of the film and with its 'message' or 'argument'. Detractors were likely to think that the preponderance of violent scenes overshadowed everything else and invalidated the film's attempt to deal with, and comment on, important issues, while some of the supporters thought that ultimately what the film had to say was rather 'opaque'.

Taking these initial critical responses to *A Clockwork Orange* as a starting point, in this part I examine some of the film's most violent scenes. I also analyse the film's beginning and its ending so as to determine more precisely how the film addresses and engages its viewers, and how it leaves them when they prepare to disengage. I want to frame my close analysis with a discussion of the film's structure, which provides the chosen scenes with a context and, through this context, with particular meanings and emotional resonances. In particular, I explore how the story's overall trajectory might influence the impact that the violent action has on the audience.

Structure and Impact I

In the long-standing scholarly debate about media violence, relatively little
attention has been paid to what would appear to be a very crucial question:
Why do people expose themselves to mediated violence? In summing up
the results of his edited collection on precisely this question, which brings
together scholars from a range of disciplines, the psychologist Jeffrey
Goldstein suggests that one of the most powerful reasons why people seek
out violent entertainment might be

> the wish to be reassured that good prevails over evil. Displays of
> violence result in distress, which is reduced when the bad guys get their
> comeuppance … [T]he typical storyline of enjoyable entertainment
> involves the establishment of animosity toward wrongdoers, which
> makes later violence against them seem justified and hence enjoyable.
> (Goldstein, 1998, p. 220)

In his contribution to Goldstein's volume, Dolf Zillmann reviews the
extensive psychological research documenting the deeply negative
responses of people confronted with violence and then focuses on one
particular mechanism which can override this negativity: 'justified hatred
and the call for punishment allows us to uninhibitedly enjoy the punitive
action when it materializes'; '[b]ecause those who help to restore social
harmony tend to be deemed purveyors of justice, their … violent action,
as it apparently serves "the common good", can be morally sanctioned'
(Zillmann, 1998, p. 202). In other words, if a narrative manages to generate
strong negative feelings in the audience against a character and sets up
the need for that character's punishment, then the audience is able to
thoroughly enjoy this punishment, even if it is very violent. Indeed, the
audience's pleasure tends to increase with the intensity of the retributive
violence, as long as that intensity is seen to be justified by the severity of the
original transgression: 'escalations in the portrayal of righteous, enjoyable

violence necessitate escalations in the portrayal of morally enraging, evil, and distressing violence' (p. 206).

From Goldstein's and Zillmann's accounts we can derive a basic narrative model for intensely enjoyable violence: first, a character who is portrayed in a very negative light – a villain – enacts extreme violence and thus disrupts the social or moral order (this section of the story distresses the audience); then, a character who is portrayed in a very positive light punishes the villain with even more extreme violence and thus restores order (this section relieves the audience of distress and gives them intense pleasure). When comparing *A Clockwork Orange* to this model, it is obvious that up to a point the film seems to be following it in an exemplary fashion, but there are also absences and reversals, which are likely to block the audience's relief and pleasure, instead intensifying their distress.[11] This helps to explain why the reviewers quoted earlier so often mention their own disgust, nausea and shock, and why even those supporting the film find their own enjoyment of it somewhat 'perverse'. Broadly speaking, we can divide *A Clockwork Orange* into three parts, the first one focusing on Alex's extremely violent behaviour, and the other two on his extended and varied punishment, first by the state, then by his former victims; in places this punishment takes extremely violent forms. At this level of analysis, the film would seem to fit the above model very well, in particular if we also consider that the audience is given very little context for Alex's initial burst of violent deeds, and certainly no explanation other than that he enjoys them, which, it could be said, characterises them as a particularly pure form of evil behaviour. However, it is also immediately obvious that, rather than introducing a positive character early on and then shifting emphasis to that character's actions against Alex, the film stays close to Alex throughout the whole story, leaving the audience no choice but to perceive his punishment mostly from his perspective, rather than from the perspective of the punitive character meting out justified violence. In addition, the film ends with the suspension of all further punishments for Alex; instead he is rewarded with a good job and perhaps even with opportunities to pursue his violent inclinations once more. If this helps to restore social order (by allowing the governing party to overcome a public-relations disaster and stay in power), then this order is obviously deeply problematic. As far as any abstract moral order is concerned, an evildoer like Alex being rewarded would appear to be the ultimate disruption, even negation of such an order (although there is more to be said about the complexities of the film's ending; see below). Thus, instead of having their confidence in justice and morality restored, at the end of the film viewers are left with the memory of brutal acts carried out by young criminals, of state-sanctioned police brutality and medical torture, of a young man driven to a suicide attempt by cynical political operators and a crazed individual looking for revenge, and with the image of a bruised, helpless body. It is not surprising that many reviewers felt sickened by the experience.

As we will see in the next section, the film's distressing impact was likely to be increased by the way individual scenes position viewers in relation to the violent and sexual action on display, and in relation to Alex.

Key Scenes

The film's story starts with a close-up of a young man in front of a black backdrop (fig. 10). He obviously wears make-up and has false eyelashes on his right eye. His clothing consists of a bowler hat, a white shirt and braces. His breathing is very noticeable, and, looking up from under the brim of his hat, he stares directly at the camera – and thus at us, the viewers. The shot is held static for seventeen seconds,[12] while the music from the credit sequence (an electronic version of Henry Purcell's *Music for the Funeral of Queen Mary*) plays on.[13] This is an unusual and indeed disturbing opening, mainly because the young man, who is supposed to be a character in a self-enclosed fictional world, acknowledges the camera, apparently aware that he is being watched by an audience. His longheld stare at the camera makes it clear that he is able to watch us in return, which suggests that there is no proper (and protective) boundary between the world of the film and the auditorium. The young

10

man's somewhat heavy breathing is ominous, as if he is either recovering from some exertion or getting ready to embark on some. What is more, his head and shoulders are disembodied and floating in blackness, and his face is made disturbingly asymmetrical as well as androgynous by his false eyelashes. In other words, he looks distinctly different from the people in the audience; he is not like us. And yet his head (of gigantic proportions when projected on a cinema screen) is also a mirror image of the way we ourselves may feel in the cinema, floating in a disembodied fashion in the blackness of the auditorium.

When, after seventeen seconds, the camera (without a cut) starts tracking backwards, the young man raises a glass to the audience with the hint of a (perhaps sardonic) smile. The backward tracking shot reveals three more young men, dressed much like the first one (with heavy black boots, tight white trousers and massive cod-pieces also now visible as well as fake eyeballs and fake wounds attached to their clothes).[14] Sitting next to him, they also look in the general direction of the camera, but in a more unfocused, absent-minded fashion. They sit at tables that are shaped like naked women spreading their legs, the hair on these women's heads as well as their pubic hair brightly coloured. To the left and the right of the young men are sculptures of more naked women, kneeling on pedestals, leaning forward and pushing out their breasts. In front of the sculpture on the right stands a bulky and muscular man, much like a guard, but dressed in body-hugging white clothes not so different from those of the four youngsters.[15] Whatever challenge or latent threat was implied in the first seventeen seconds of this shot has been enhanced with the beginning of the camera's backward movement, because, although some distance is placed between ourselves and the first young man, he once again explicitly acknowledges us by raising his glass to us. In addition, we realise that we have to contend not only with him but also with three others just like him. Their being completely at ease in an environment that most of us would probably find obscene and disturbing is also not a good sign.

About a minute into the opening shot, with the camera still tracking backwards, the young man we first saw introduces himself in a voiceover as Alex. He also identifies his 'droogs' (Pete, Georgie and Dim), their location (the Korova Milk Bar) and his drink ('milk-plus', that is, we presume, milk with some added stimulant), and states that they are 'trying to make up our rassoodocks what to do with the evening'. The backward tracking reveals a long, corridor-like room. Alex and his droogs sit at one end, and at the sides, there are more people, some of them wearing clothes similar to Alex's. They sit at tables which are also shaped like women spreading their legs and thrusting their pelvises towards the camera and, in between these tables there are more pedestals with sculptures of naked women. The backward tracking shot eventually reveals two more bulky men standing guard near the edges of the frame at the end of the two rows of tables and pedestals (fig. 11). After Alex's voiceover has declared that 'milk-plus' 'make[s] you ready for a bit of the old ultra-violence', the tracking movement and with it the scene (a single shot lasting for just over one and a half minutes) ends. This final section of the opening shot works towards confirming the threat posed by Alex and his droogs, and, by featuring a slang which is completely alien to us (although we can guess the meaning of the words), it also confirms the radical otherness of these young men. From the outset, their fake eyeballs and wounds have

11

suggested a potential for violence, and so we are perhaps not surprised that when they try to make up their minds about what to do that evening, they decide on 'ultra-violence', whereby the adjective 'old' indicates that they are very familiar with such violence, that they have indulged in it on many previous evenings.

The film's second scene starts with a medium shot of the mid-section of a man (he is headless where Alex's head at the beginning of the first shot was disembodied), lying on the ground, holding a bottle and singing a song. The camera zooms out, revealing that the man lies in an underpass and is approached by four people who cast ominous shadows in his direction. After thirty-five seconds of the man and his singing dominating the shot, Alex's voiceover starts. A reverse shot then shows four silhouetted figures walking towards the man. When Alex's voiceover has expressed his disgust for drunks, especially old ones, the film cuts from an extreme long shot to a regular long shot, showing the droogs mostly in profile, with their cod-pieces hanging out. They laugh and applaud the man, who has stopped singing and is now asking them for money, to which Alex responds by ramming the stick he is carrying into his stomach. Their subsequent interaction is shown in alternating shots:

two medium long shots roughly from Alex's point of view, looking down on the man on the ground, and two tight close-ups of Alex in profile (figs. 12–13). The man's dialogue puts Alex's attack on him in the wider context of a society where 'there's no law and order any more', a society that 'lets the young get onto the old'. When the man starts singing again, the second tight close-up of Alex has him swinging his stick so as to be able to whack him really hard.

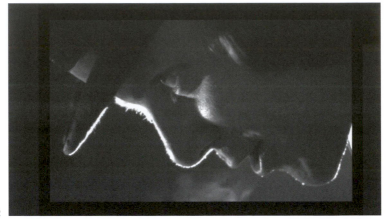

12

13

The film cuts back to a long shot showing all four droogs hitting the man with sticks and chains, and kicking him; the shot lasts only eight seconds, but feels longer. As in the opening scene, more or less symmetrical shot compositions dominate in this second scene, and the camera is mostly at a considerable distance from the characters. The violent action is depicted in a stylised fashion. When Alex initially pushes his stick into the drunk's belly, the latter does not scream in pain but embarks on a speech about the state of the world, and the all-out attack at the end is shown in a silhouetted long shot. The impact of boots and sticks and chains on the man's body remains invisible and once again there are no screams of pain, only the sounds of objects making contact with the man's body, and the excited and joyful shrieking of the droogs. If this scene is disturbing, it is so, less because of the physical violence we actually see, and more because of the enjoyment the droogs get out of it and our own temporary optical affiliation with their leader. In two shots we almost take Alex's place, looking down along the stick with which he pins his victim to the ground.

Whereas the violence of the attempted rape and the gang fight in Scene 3 is mostly presented in (extreme) long shots and in a balletic fashion, with the camera being at a distance both from the action and from Alex's point of view, in Scene 4 the viewer is frequently taking Alex's place behind the wheels of the stolen car, rushing forward with it and seeing the vehicles that are being forced off the road from Alex's point of view. This time his victims remain altogether invisible. However, the scene ends with a close-up of Alex staring directly at the camera (as he did at the beginning of the film's first scene), while his voiceover announces 'the old surprise visit', with 'lashings of the old ultra-violence' (fig. 14), which is reminiscent of the end of the first scene. Scene 5 starts with two extreme long shots of the car arriving at a house and its passengers sneaking up on 'Home'. Comparable to the opening of Scene 2, the film then concentrates on Mr and Mrs Alexander, the prospective victims of the threatened and promised 'ultra-violence', for about a minute, before Alex and his droogs invade the house, their cod-pieces and sticks being complemented by the huge, phallic noses of their masks. The subsequent

14

violent action is mostly presented in long shot. There are no closer shots of
sticks, boots and hands making contact with the victims' bodies, no images
of bruises or cuts, and the victims' screams of pain are largely drowned out by
Alex's singing as well as the shrieks and laughter of his droogs, and then they
are muffled when the Alexanders are gagged. While their physical suffering
could thus be said to be played down, Mr Alexander's mental anguish is
increasingly pushed to the fore.

Within twenty seconds of the invaders entering the house, a medium
shot briefly shows his face when, lying on the ground and being held down
by Georgie, he confusedly asks: 'What do you want from me?' About forty
seconds later, another medium shot shows a ball being shoved in his mouth
and sticky tape being wrapped around his head. About eighty seconds after
the invaders enter – which is also eighty seconds before this scene ends – the
camera is positioned close to the ground behind Mr Alexander's head, looking
up, much like Mr Alexander does, at his wife being placed by Dim in front of
Alex. From now on, the film cuts back and forth between medium close-ups
of Mr Alexander's grossly distorted face, his eyes appearing to pop out of his
head, and low-angle long shots, taken from behind Mr Alexander, which

show what happens to his wife (figs. 15–16). Alex cuts out holes in her dress around her breasts, and then cuts away all of her clothes, so that she is finally as exposed as the plastic women in Scene 1, with the red hair on her head and her red pubic hair just as much on display as the coloured hair of those plastic women had been. Early on, a low-angle, medium close-up of Mrs Alexander is inserted into this shot sequence in order to highlight her distress which in

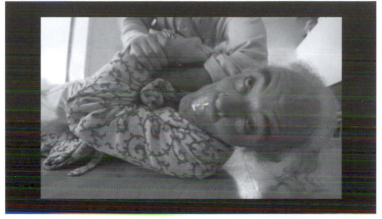

15

16

¹⁷

turn gives the medium close-ups of her husband an additional emotional
charge. Towards the end of the scene, Alex drops his trousers and walks
towards Mr Alexander, kneeling down in front of him. The next medium
close-up of Mr Alexander has Alex's phallic nose entering the frame from
the top and then his whole head. The reverse shot taken exactly from Mr
Alexander's position shows Alex looking directly at him – and thus at the
camera and the audience: 'Viddy well, little brother. Viddy well' ('Watch
carefully') (fig. 17). Alex then jumps up and moves towards Mrs Alexander.
This is followed by another medium close-up of Mr Alexander and another
medium shot of Mrs Alexander, writhing painfully while Alex appears to be
grappling with the lower half of her body. With this shot, which represents Mr
Alexander's perspective on his wife's suffering, the scene ends.

Rather than being optically aligned with Alex, as they had been
temporarily in Scenes 2 and 4, here the viewers are not only placed in the
position of one of the victims, but they are also directly addressed as viewers
by Alex ('Viddy well', he tells us). Since viewing the humiliation of, and the
sexual attack on, his wife is painful for her husband, it is likely to be
particularly unpleasant for the audience as well. Throughout this scene, the

camera observes Alex's actions at a distance, never taking up his position or perspective (with the exception of the penultimate medium close-up of Mr Alexander, which is taken roughly from where Alex was at the end of the previous shot, but does not represent his point of view because he pushes his face into the frame). Thus, while we have occasionally been given a taste of what it might feel like to be in Alex's place in the film's first five scenes, by and large, Alex and his violence have been kept at a distance from us, and the most extended violent scene has placed us firmly on the side of his victims. In addition, throughout these opening scenes, Alex has repeatedly looked directly at the camera, thus challenging and threatening us, but also perhaps reminding us that we are watching a movie. This does not mean that we are safe, because we know from Mr Alexander's experience that, even if one is physically removed from the action, merely watching it and listening to it can be unbearable (an observation which will later underpin the Ludovico treatment). Thus, in addition to obscene displays of the female body and the relentless violence of Alex and his droogs, it is the viewer's shifting position – sometimes challenged and threatened by Alex, at other times optically aligned and perhaps emotionally complicit with him, sometimes observing the action from a distance and at other times taking the place of a victim who in turn is observing the victimisation of a loved one – which can be expected to cause severe distress in the audience across the film's first five scenes.

For this distress to be relieved and converted into enjoyment, Alex needs to be punished, according to Goldstein's and Zillmann's model. Yet, when this punishment finally comes, after eleven more scenes, many of which are filled with more obscenity and violence, much of it is shown with the camera – and thus the viewer – placed in Alex's position. Scene 17 at the police station ends with a shot/reverse shot sequence (almost two minutes long) which alternates high-angle shots of Alex lying on the ground and looking up, his body covered in blood, with low-angle medium long shots of three policemen and Mr Deltoid looking down on him. The latter represent Alex's optical point of view, which means that now it is not Alex, but his victimisers who stare directly into the camera. The scene concludes with

18

Deltoid moving closer to the camera and addressing it – and us – directly (fig. 18); referring to the death of the woman Alex attacked, he says: 'I hope to God it will torture you to madness.' Deltoid is getting ready to spit at Alex, and the scene ends with a close-up of his face being covered in saliva. Throughout this extended shot/reverse shot sequence, the camera repeatedly puts us exactly in Alex's position, while its optical alignment with the policemen and Deltoid is not exact: Alex is never looking directly at the camera, and in his last two close-ups, we can see parts of Deltoid's head at the edges of the frame. Thus, when Alex at the end tries to reassert himself by staring defiantly and with the hint of a smile at Deltoid, his stare is no longer aimed directly at us (fig. 19). From now on, rather than feeling challenged by his stare and by what he does, we are invited to share his experiences, especially his 'tortures' and most especially the tortures inflicted upon him by being put in the position of someone who helplessly watches, and listens to, scenes of violence. Of course, this is the position occupied by Mr Alexander – and through our alignment with him, by us – in Scene 5. In a more general sense, this has been our position all along, as spectators (and listeners) being confronted with a distressing movie, a parallel which the Ludovico treatment

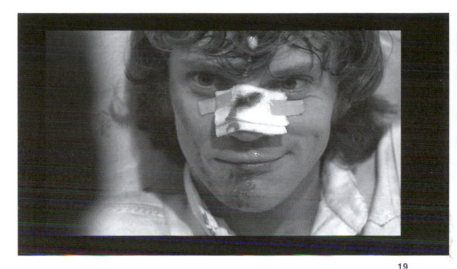

19

makes explicit: Not only do the scenes in which Alex is shown violent films put us optically in his position, but they also put Alex in the very position which we have occupied since the film's violent action started in Scene 2.

Let's now think once again about how all of this fits into the structure of the film and into its overall narrative trajectory.

Structure and Impact II

If, as suggested earlier, we take the presence of Alex's criminal violence and of his punishment as our guide, we can identify the following three parts of roughly equal length. Part 1, consisting of Scenes 1–16 (with a combined length of 42:45 min), focuses largely on Alex's violent behaviour, and Part 2 (Scenes 17–28, 44:34 min) on official responses to Alex's crimes and their impact on his body and mind; these responses range from police brutality in Scene 17 to his imprisonment in Scenes 18–22 and his subjection to the Ludovico treatment, which culminates in a cruel public display, in Scenes 23–8.[16] Part 3 (Scenes 29–40, 45:44 min) focuses on unofficial punitive responses to Alex's crimes and their impact on his body and mind: Alex is rejected by his parents and several of his former victims take revenge on him, as a consequence of which he ends up in hospital, where he remains at the end of the film, still in plaster and in pain.

Individual incidents featuring Alex's violence in Part 1 are echoed in the other two parts with Alex now in the role of the victim. Thus, the attack on the tramp in Scene 2 is replayed in the first film Alex sees during the Ludovico treatment in Scene 25 (showing four youths beating up a man), which begins to make Alex feel unwell. His first victim then takes revenge on Alex in Scene 30, rallying a group of fellow tramps who beat Alex up (with several shots taken from Alex's point of view). The sexual attack on Mrs Alexander in Scene 5 is replayed in the second film of the Ludovico treatment showing a woman being gang-raped by several youths, which makes Alex feel very sick indeed. Mr Alexander then takes revenge on Alex in Scene 35, driving him to a suicide attempt. Such repetitions lend themselves to the dynamic described by Goldstein (1998) and Zillmann (1998), whereby punishment of an initial transgression can be very satisfying for the audience. Yet this is unlikely to happen here. Whereas Alex is almost continuously on screen, the two characters taking revenge on him are off screen for most of the film, making it difficult for viewers to get involved in their side of the story. Instead the audience is drawn deeper and deeper into Alex's experience, not least, as we have seen, by the camera's optical alignment with him.

An important aspect of Alex's experience, which is likely to make him appear more sympathetic, or at least more pathetic, in the viewers' eyes, is his rejection by those closest to him: his parents, the members of his gang and his 'Post Corrective Adviser'. With regards to his droogs, this rejection plays out in an extremely violent fashion. First, Alex hitting and cutting Dim (in Scenes 6 and 14) leads to Dim hitting and cutting Alex in the face with a milk bottle (in Scene 16); then, Scene 14, which has both Dim and Georgie being thrown into water, is spectacularly replayed in Scene 31, when the two dunk Alex in a trough, beating and almost drowning him. While Mr Deltoid is not portrayed as a particularly friendly or supportive character, he describes himself – probably correctly – as 'the one man in this sore and sick community who wants to save you from yourself' (Scene 10). Later (Scene 17) when Deltoid spits in Alex's face at the police station, he does so with a crazed grin; however, his disappointment in Alex, his disgust at his crimes is understandable. Least spectacular, yet perhaps most devastating, is Alex's rejection by his parents. Initially, it is Alex who keeps them at a distance; he does not open his bedroom door for his mother when she wakes him up for school (Scene 9). Yet, when he comes out of prison, his first port of call is his parents' flat, and the realisation that he cannot return to live with them, indeed that he appears to have been replaced in their affections by another young man, makes him cry (Scene 29). He storms out with a veiled threat: 'You won't viddy me no more. … Let it lie heavy on your consciences.' In the very next scene, he walks along the riverbank and a point-of-view shot indicates not only that he stares intently at the water, but by zooming in on a spot beneath the bridge, suggests that Alex's mind is fixating on the river, perhaps on the idea of drowning himself in it. This is later confirmed when, shortly before jumping out of the window in Scene 35, Alex reveals in his voiceover: 'Suddenly, I viddied what I had to do, and what I had wanted to do, and that was to do myself in.' Thus, it would appear that it is not the Ludovico treatment – and Alex's inability to enjoy violence, sex and Beethoven's *Ninth* – that initially makes him feel suicidal, but the withdrawal of his parents' support and love.

Hence, a key element among the many reversals towards the end of the film is the parents' visit to the hospital (Scene 38). Although Alex indicates that they are not welcome, in a longheld point-of-view shot we see his father talking directly at the camera, accepting partial responsibility for what happened to Alex and offering support: 'Your home's your home when all's said and done, son' (fig. 20). This emphasis on the word 'home' echoes across the film as a whole. The sign in front of the Alexanders' house reads 'Home' (Scenes 5 and 32), and when, after having cruelly invaded and devastated this home, Alex approaches it again at what is another low point in his life – rejected by his parents, beaten up by his old friends – his voiceover states:

20

Where was I to go, who had no home and no money? I cried for myself. Home, home, home. It was home I was wanting and it was Home I came to, brothers, not realising in the state I was in, where I was and had been before.

The incessant repetition of the word 'home' expresses his most deeply felt desire and also perhaps a recognition of the severity of his previous attacks on homes. Indeed, when, in Scene 39, the psychiatrist shows him a slide of a man on a ladder about to enter a naked woman's bedroom, his response to her worried question ('What do you want?') is: 'No time for the old in-out, love. I've just come to read the meter.' Although it is meant as a joke, when set against the backdrop of his two home invasions with their sexualised attacks on women (both of whom die), there is perhaps a certain respect for the sanctity of other people's homes and the inviolability of a woman's body at work here. This would seem to be confirmed by Alex's final fantasy, in which he appears to have consensual and mutually satisfying sex with a woman. It is also worth noting that in Scene 30, after having been brought to an extremely low point by his parents' rejection and the loss of his home, Alex, acting without any thought, perhaps out of a newly found understanding of human suffering and the necessity of mutual support, shows generosity towards the tramp who asks him for money.

The idea that, from Scene 29 onwards, Alex is suffering from the lack of parental support and a home, and is desperately looking for both, while also beginning to show some compassion, puts his dealings with the Minister of the Interior (who is the fictional equivalent, one assumes, of the real-world 'Home Secretary') in the final scene in a different light. Like Deltoid, this is not a sympathetic character, yet, for reasons of political expediency and self-protection, he does treat Alex in a friendly, indeed parental fashion. When he arrives, he addresses Alex as 'my boy', shows concern for his well-being and then even starts feeding the helpless young man. He assures Alex that from now on he will take care of him, so that Alex 'will have no worries'. Importantly, Alex is interested in the particulars of the minister's promise of 'a good job on a good salary': 'What job and how much?' This contrasts sharply with the way he privileged the enjoyment of criminal acts over the money to be 'earned' with them in the dispute with his droogs in Scene 13: 'And what will you do with the big, big, big money? Have you not everything you need?' Georgie's response has the ring of truth: 'Brother, you think and talk sometimes like a little child.' By showing interest in his future job and earnings, in Scene 40, Alex indicates that he is now able to think in more mature (and less criminal) ways. This more mature thinking also seems to underpin the deal he is prepared to make with the minister who expects some help from Alex: 'We always help our friends, don't we?' Alex agrees: 'You can rely on me, sir.' While these are the same words he used disingenuously in his conversation with Deltoid in Scene 10, it is entirely possible that this time he means them – because, having lost everything once, he is now more careful about having the support of others. Indeed he is immediately rewarded for his promise, when the minister gives him a present 'as a symbol of our new understanding, an understanding between two friends'. We last see the Minister putting his arm around Alex and proudly presenting him and their 'friendship' to the world (looking directly at the camera), and Alex plays along,

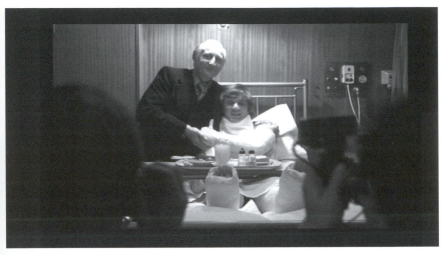

21

smiling and raising his thumb (fig. 21), before he drifts off into a fantasy of sex and public approval. In this context, Alex's last statement – 'I was cured all right' – resonates deeply and widely, encompassing his ability once again to enjoy the *Ninth* and sexual fantasy, his new friendship, the support both of the government and of his parents, and also perhaps of the public at large. In so many ways, Alex is 'home' again.

Conclusion

The first part of *A Clockwork Orange* is designed to distress viewers, not only by exposing them to violent action and obscene displays of the female body, but also by aligning viewers optically with Alex or with his victims. Brief alignments with Alex suggest the viewers' complicity with his deeds, while longer alignments with his victims intensify feelings of horror, fear and disgust. In response to Alex's transgressive behaviour in the first part of *A Clockwork Orange*, the second and third part of the film feature not only a rich catalogue of punishments (ranging from imprisonment to being rejected by his parents) but also foreground the depths of Alex's suffering and hint at a fundamental, perhaps redemptive shift in his attitude towards the world, which now includes some compassion, a more mature and pragmatic concern for jobs and salaries, as well as, quite possibly, an emphasis on sexual pleasure rather than the sadistic pleasures of violence. Depending on how affected we are by our exposure to Alex's suffering, and how receptive we are to these hints of redemption, Alex being freed from the restrictions of the Ludovico treatment, regaining the support and love of his parents and finding a new 'friend', might even appear to have some justification. Yet the film certainly does not make it easy for us to believe in Alex's redemption and thus to perceive his extraordinary punishments as necessary and transformative, rather than cruel and destructive. What is more, the fact that we consistently experience these punishments (as well as the final rewards) of Parts 2 and 3 from Alex's perspective makes it impossible for us to find the kind of pleasurable release from the distressing impact of mediated violence which, according to Goldstein (1998) and Zillmann (1998), is usually offered in popular stories through retributive violence.

So where does all this leave the audience at the end? The last we see of Alex is a close-up. In contrast to his challenging and threatening stare at the camera when we first encountered him at the beginning of this story, now he looks upwards and perhaps inwards, his facial expression going all soft due to the impact, we assume, of his internal visions (fig. 22). The next shot, which is the final shot of the film's story, shows us what he is seeing with his mind's eye, which means that, rather than finding ourselves opposite Alex, we have now become one with him as indeed we had done on numerous previous occasions when we entered his fantasy world. This is no longer a question of optical point of view because in our fantasies we can be both agents in a scene and disembodied observers roaming around in that scene. The people lining the sides of this eighteen-second long shot form a kind of corridor (fig. 23), which echoes the presentation of the Korova Milk Bar at the film's beginning. Now, Alex (if the young man in the snow is indeed Alex; it is impossible to tell) is positioned in the foreground of the shot rather than at the end of the corridor.

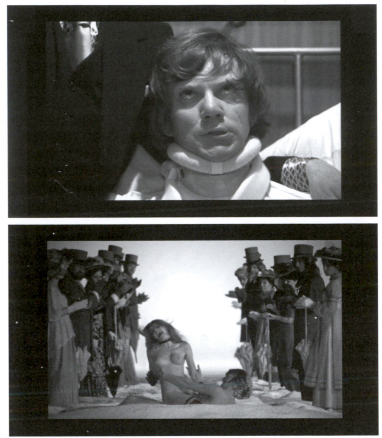

22

23

The plastic female nudes of the Korova Milk Bar have given way to a flesh-and-blood woman who sits astride Alex, naked, with her mouth open, writhing and apparently enjoying herself, but also seemingly pushing away his hands which are trying to grab her, and leaning backwards, away from him. This is a reminder of Alex's previous fantasies about, and experiences of, consensual sex (the threesome in Scene 12, laying with the 'handmaidens' in his bible fantasies in Scene 20), but it also, of course, refers back both to his sexual attack on Mrs

Alexander in Scene 5 and to his inability to even touch the naked woman presented to him on a stage in Scene 28. The anachronistically dressed people on the sides of this final shot applaud, which is reminiscent of the applause Alex receives in Scene 28 after it has been demonstrated that he has successfully completed the Ludovico treatment (and perhaps of the press photographers who take pictures of Alex after he has fully recovered from the treatment). The applause also relates back to Alex clapping his hands in response to the drunk's singing in Scene 2 which preceded a brutal attack.

The musical accompaniment of, and indeed the inspiration for, this final fantasy – Beethoven's *Ninth Symphony* – resonates across much of the film, evoking Alex's enjoyment of a woman singing the 'Ode to Joy' and his anger about Dim's disruption of it in Scene 6, Alex's violent fantasies inspired by the *Ninth* in Scene 8, his terror and anger when he realises that the *Ninth* accompanies propaganda and war films shown to him during the Ludovico treatment in Scene 27, his unbearable suffering driving him to a suicide attempt in Scene 35. Similarly, once this final shot of the story has come to an end and the credits begin, Gene Kelly's performance of 'Singin' in the Rain' evokes both Alex's invasion and devastation of the Alexanders' home, but also an illusory moment of peace, when Alex has returned 'Home' and sings while enjoying a bath, thus inadvertently revealing himself to his previous victim in Scene 33. At the same time, because it is now Gene Kelly singing the song rather than Alex/Malcolm McDowell, we are also reminded of one of Hollywood's most beloved musicals and a transcendent moment of love, exhilaration and joy, which raises the question of whether this moment will now forever be spoilt for us by its association with Alex's brutal attack, or whether we can transcend this association in the same way that Gene Kelly is able to transcend bad weather by turning it into a celebration of life ('What a glorious feeling / I'm happy again') and also like Alex who has finally overcome his aversive response to Beethoven's *Ninth Symphony* and sex ('I was cured all right').

It would appear that in many ways the film's ending is wide open so that, depending on what we bring to *A Clockwork Orange*, at its conclusion we can take away from it all kinds of ideas about Alex's current state of mind and his plans for the future, a range of feelings about him, his past deeds and suffering and his present joy, a wide variety of responses to the film as a whole, its themes, form and style. In Part 3, I examine how this film – and in particular its ending – came about.

# PART 3

PRODUCTION HISTORY

Introduction

At the beginning of 1963, Anthony Burgess's novel *A Clockwork Orange* was widely and often very positively reviewed in the American press. Almost all critics highlighted the 'invented language' in which the novel's first-person narrator, Alex, relates his tale (Moran, 1963). It was described as a 'yet-to-come brand of teen-age jargon' (Boucher, 1963), which was extrapolated from 'present-day English "Teddy-Boy" slang' (*Analog*, 1963). There was a lot of praise for the 'Joycean' inventiveness and brilliance of Burgess's writing (Yudkin, 1963) but also some concern that it might 'act as a barrier to the general reader' (Moran, 1963). There was uncertainty about how best to describe the impact of the book's language, one reviewer claiming that due to its lack of familiar 'overtones' and 'emotional connotations', 'the reader has little or no emotional response' to the 'most horrible scenes and events' in the story; '[a]t the same time, the words set one's teeth on edge' (*Register Magazine*, 1963). Another reviewer argued that Alex's 'artificial slang has an emotional impact which transcends specific word meanings'; he compared it to 'the music which rouses Alex to passion' (Talbot, 1963). Indeed, one critic suggested, most probably not altogether seriously, that Alex's slang – and with it also certain aspects of his behaviour – could 'be taken up by some adolescents. If someday someone calls you an "old veck", watch out!' (*Register Magazine*, 1963). After all, the language was intimately linked with extremely transgressive behaviour: 'The endless sadistic violence in the book, unimaginably nasty, mindless and mind-hating, is described by Alex with eloquence and joy' (Hyman, 1963); '[t]he story moves along rapidly and keeps you smiling even while heads are being bashed in and stomachs kicked' (Zotigh, 1963).

Many critics noted the close links between the fictional world the book described and the realities of contemporary society: 'The teen-age world of

Alex and his gang is unrelievedly evil by our standards although it is all too like the headlines in almost any big-city newspaper' (*Analog*, 1963). In particular, the novel was said to mirror the real-life problem of juvenile delinquency while also building on popular representations of this problem (notably the 1955 movie *Rebel without a Cause*). The novel told the 'story of the reform of a juvenile delinquent' (Moran, 1963) and Alex was labelled 'a juvenile super-delinquent' (Boucher, 1963), 'the ultimate delinquent, the last of a succession of sallow-faced rebels without a cause' (Talbot, 1963). One reviewer thought that, '[f]or those disturbed by the acts of violence committed by certain members of the younger generation', the novel 'offers a frightening insight into the probable thinking of the violent young' (*Berkeley Gazette*, 1963). While these American commentators thus related *A Clockwork Orange* to contemporary America, they also distanced it from their own society by making it very clear that the novel was set in a futuristic England (although they could not agree whether it was only a few years in the future or several decades). Critics noted that the novel's portrayal of juvenile delinquency was based on the British 'Teddy Boy' phenomenon, with Alex being described as 'a music-appreciating, child-molesting teddy boy' (*Berkeley Gazette*, 1963).

More generally, despite the fact that the country in which the novel's action takes place is never identified, American writers found it easier to associate its vision of a society ruled by a powerful government which interferes in all aspects of individual and social life with Britain than with the US. Hence they described *A Clockwork Orange* as 'a dazzling indictment of the welfare state' (Tucker, 1963), which in turn was underpinned by 'a limp and listless socialism' (Hyman, 1963). In the view of these writers, Britain seemed already well on the way to developing into the kind of society portrayed in the novel, 'a sick society from which has been purged all notion of individual responsibility' (Stanley, 1963), a 'society [that] turns men into automatons', indeed 'a clockwork society' (Talbot, 1963): '[Alex's] dreary socialist England is a giant clockwork orange' (Hyman, 1963). Hence, when many of these critics described the novel as a 'moral fable' and 'social satire' reminiscent of George Orwell's *Nineteen Eighty-Four* (1949), they ultimately appeared to see

Communism and its influence on 'socialist' European governments as its main target (even if conservative parties were in charge). This association was probably strengthened by the fact that Alex's language used 'dozens of Russian words' (Talbot, 1963) and that the 'totalitarian' 'Ludovico Technique' of 'brainwashing' featured in the novel also had a distinctly Eastern European ring to it (*Springfield Republican*, 1963).

While some reviews noted the novel's theological dimension (its 'intention is Christian', according to Hyman, 1963; cp. Yeiser, 1963), American critics tended to see it as a social and/or political allegory. *A Clockwork Orange* was a warning about the threat criminal youth posed to the social order (e.g. Stanley, 1963), or about the totalitarian tendencies of modern governments (e.g. Tucker, 1963, and *Berkeley Gazette*, 1963), or indeed both (e.g. *Analog*, 1963). The more political a writer's approach was, the more Alex emerged from the review as an ultimately sympathetic character who resists totalitarian domination: Alex and his droogs are 'the most vital, twisted members in a sick society' (Stanley, 1963); '[h]is crimes are the only positive acts in a negative landscape of robot people', which means that 'in a clockwork society, human redemption will have to arise out of evil' (Talbot, 1963). In this way, the novel's ending (with Alex declaring 'I was cured all right') could be perceived as a kind of triumph: overcoming the 'annihilation of his soul' (Tucker, 1963), 'Alex returns to his former self' (Yudkin, 1963); 'he will rob and murder …, unless he wills otherwise, for he is a human being again' (Thorpe, 1963). Alex shaking off the effects of the Ludovico treatment did not necessarily mean that he would return to his old ways; instead he had regained the power to choose good or evil, and, as far as at least some of the reviewers were concerned, the novel left it open which way he might go. Little did these critics know that the novel's original British edition, which by and large was not well received by British reviewers (Biswell, 2005, pp. 258–60), contained an extra chapter showing that Alex simply grows out of his evil ways.

In this part, I first discuss the origins of Burgess's novel and how it came to have two endings. I then outline the various attempts made by American as well as British writers and filmmakers, building on the novel's positive reception in the US, to turn it into a movie during the 1960s and why they failed. Finally I examine why Kubrick became involved and how he adapted the novel.

The Novel

By the time he embarked on *A Clockwork Orange* in spring 1961, Anthony Burgess had written several, often very autobiographical novels, an English literature textbook and numerous newspaper and magazine articles.[17] He had only recently begun to make a living from his writing; before that he had been a schoolteacher, first in Britain, where he had been born near Manchester in 1917, and then, from 1954 in Malaysia and Borneo. Upon his return to the UK in 1959, Burgess was highly sensitised to changes that had taken place in this country during the five years in which he had largely been away (with the exception of brief visits). His biographer Andrew Biswell notes that '[o]ne of the central preoccupations in the novels he wrote around this time is the extent to which England had altered – and not, apparently, for the better – between 1954 and 1959' (Biswell, 2005, p. 224). This included, among many other things, what he saw as the negative American influence on the musical taste and film preferences, the language, attitudes and behaviour of British people, especially youth (p. 224). With *A Clockwork Orange*, Burgess aimed to project such developments into the future so as to explore where they might lead. Biswell is sceptical about many of the details of the stories Burgess later told about how *A Clockwork Orange* was a response to the attack on his wife during the war (cp. my discussion of this in the Introduction) and about a cancer diagnosis he received in 1959, giving him only a short time to live, in response to which he quickly wrote several novels, including *A Clockwork Orange* (Biswell, 2005, pp. 107–9, 204–13). Rather than relating the novel to uncertain personal circumstances, critics have found it more productive to reconstruct the literary models Burgess was drawing on and the developments in British society he was engaging with.[18]

Most obviously, *A Clockwork Orange* – and also the second dystopian novel Burgess published in 1962 (*The Wanting Seed*) – was heavily influenced by two classics of British dystopian literature, Aldous Huxley's *Brave New World* (1932) and George Orwell's *Nineteen Eighty-Four*.[19] While developing similar themes and taking over quite a few ideas from his literary predecessors, Burgess was applying them very specifically to the social, cultural and political realities of 1950s and early 1960s Britain. Rob Spence shows, for example, that the depiction of youth culture in *A Clockwork Orange*, with its emphasis on 'milk bars' and what appears to be largely foreign pop music (Alex's taste for classical music being an exception among his peers), echoes – and perhaps directly drew on – Richard Hoggart's classic 1957 study of post-war British working-class culture, *The Uses of Literacy*, with its particular concern about the influence of American culture on young people especially (Spence, 2009, p. 41; Hoggart, 1957). More generally, the novel's focus on the 'nadsat' age group, that is 'teenagers' (a term which had only fairly recently come into widespread use), on their importance as consumers, the distinctiveness and changeability of their tastes (especially in music and fashion), their sexual precocity and their delinquency mirrored developments in 50s British society and the heated public debates about these developments.[20]

While I am not in a position to relate particular elements of *A Clockwork Orange* to specific encounters Burgess may have had with British youth or other aspects of British life, or to the books and newspapers he may have read about his home country while living abroad, it is nevertheless reasonable to assume that he was fully aware of key developments and debates in Britain during this period. When compared to the drastic changes in British (and American) society during the 1960s and 1970s, the first fifteen years after World War II are often seen as a period of stability, characterised by comparatively high levels of social cohesion and cultural homogeneity as well as relatively low levels of crime and political conflict. However, for people living through this period – such as Anthony Burgess – there were plenty of dramatic developments to get excited or worried about. For example, the number of rape cases in England and Wales more than doubled between 1951 and 1961, as did the number of such cases reported in national newspapers (Soothill and Walby, 1991, pp. 18–21). Stories about particular crimes or about the criminal-justice system made up around 10% of all newspaper articles in the late 1940s and the 1950s (a percentage that would increase in subsequent decades), and an astonishing 20% of all films released in Britain during this period, including many box-office hits, focused on crime (this percentage remained stable in subsequent decades) (Reiner, Livingstone and Allen, 2000, pp. 112–13). After a decade of minor ups and downs, from the mid-1950s onwards the number of all offences reported by the police soared; it had doubled by the early 1960s (Maguire, 2002, pp. 344–5). A criminological study about London, published in the mid-1950s, reported that numerous crimes were committed by juveniles working in organised 'gangs' or, more frequently, in unstructured and fleeting associations; typically such groups consisted of three to five boys, most of whom were in their early teens.[21] From 1954 onwards, juvenile misbehaviour and delinquency became closely associated in the press with so-called 'Teddy Boys'.[22] These were young, working-class males who had adopted middle- and upper-class 'Edwardian' suits as well as American music and slang, and were reported to be involved in, among many other things, 'gang' fights and 'riots' at cinemas, especially when American rock'n'roll films were shown.

Much of this found its way, in an exaggerated fashion, into Burgess's novel: Alex's gang is uniformed 'in the height of fashion' (Burgess, 1962/1972, p. 5); 'the teaming up [in gangs] was mostly by fours or fives' (p. 15); newspapers report 'the usual about ultra-violence and bank robberies' (p. 34) and feature 'articles on Modern Youth' which try to explain its delinquency and what can be done about it (p. 35); at the centre of all this is a vicious young criminal who, it is revealed after a third of the book, is 'still only fifteen' (p. 60). The novel's extrapolation from developments in 50s British film culture is particularly interesting. After their confrontation with Billyboy's gang, Alex and his friends steal a car from the car park of 'the filthy old Filmdrome, peeling and dropping to bits through nobody going there much except malchiks [boys] like me and my droogs' (p. 18). When Burgess was writing this, cinema attendance had entered a period of catastrophic decline. Annual ticket sales dropped almost 70% between their historical peak in 1946 and 1960; the steepest decline took place between 1956 and 1960, with ticket sales in 1960 being less than half of what they had been four years earlier (Hanson, 2007, pp. 92–3). The cinema audience was dominated by urban working-class youth, who bought more than half of all tickets in the late 1940s and saw their share increasing across the next decade (Docherty, Morrison and Tracey, 1987, pp. 17, 27). Alex's comments on the 'Filmdrome' capture nicely where this development might lead.

In his novel, Burgess also played on the public debates which surrounded this close association between cinema and working-class youth (although we should not forget that the biggest UK box-office hits of the period were historical epics and musicals addressed to a cross-class family audience; Hall, 1999, esp. vol. 2, pp. 145–6). From autumn 1956 onwards, there were numerous newspaper reports about young people – variously identified as 'Teddy Boys', 'hooligans' or 'teenagers' – who behaved disruptively during screenings of American films like *Rock around the Clock* (1956) and *Don't Knock the Rock* (1956); they were clapping, dancing, throwing things at the screen, slashing seats and getting into fights with the police.[23] According to the press, such behaviour, initially focused on rock'n'roll movies, which dealt with generational conflict (mostly around musical taste) and featured young people enjoying themselves at rock'n'roll performances, later spread to screenings of other kinds of films, with numerous articles about this issue appearing as late as 1961.[24] Public debates about cinema 'riots' were informed by the idea that the behaviour of youth audiences could be understood as a response to the behaviour of young characters in the films, so that the latter's exuberant and disruptive action on screen translated into rioting in the auditorium. Together with anxieties about 'Americanisation' and about the general moral decline of youth, the idea that young people were inclined to copy what they saw in the cinema also underpinned the harsh treatment of juvenile-delinquency movies such as *Rebel without a Cause* and *Blackboard Jungle* (1955) by the British Board of Film Censors (BBFC) in the 1950s.[25]

In *A Clockwork Orange*, Burgess built on the intense public debate about the negative effects of films about youth on young viewers as well as on Orwell's idea (in *Nineteen Eighty-Four*) of the 'Two Minutes Hates', daily film screenings which whip their audiences into '[a] hideous ecstasy of fear and vindictiveness, a desire to kill, to torture, to smash faces with a sledge-hammer' (p. 15). However, the novel's 'Ludovico Technique' reverses the direction in which films (with a little help from drugs) influence their viewers. Rather than imitating what he sees, Alex is programmed never to engage in violent behaviour again, never even to contemplate it, because instead of his previous enjoyment of screen (and real) violence he now finds it unbearable. Many of the films he watches are precisely about 'grinning and smecking malchicks in the heighth of nadsat fashion', that is male teenagers such as himself, behaving badly (Burgess, 1962/1972, p. 93; cp. pp. 82, 88–9). In other words, this juvenile delinquent is turned around – 'impelled towards the good' (p. 99) – precisely by juvenile-delinquency movies.

The key role played by drugs in the Ludovico treatment – and also in the spiked milk drinks that people consume in the novel (their mind-altering impact being described in some detail in Chapter 1) – is reminiscent of the centrality of various forms of biochemical manipulation (including both the state's medical treatment of embryos and people's self-medication with the happiness drug Soma) in Huxley's *Brave New World*. At the same time, Burgess is likely to have been aware of the varied uses of drugs in the 1940s and 1950s: as stimulants for creative people, as elements in the treatment of sex offenders and as components in so-called 'brainwashing' (a term coined in 1950) of foreigners, dissidents and prisoners of war by Chinese, Soviet and North Korean Communists.[26] All of these received a considerable amount of attention in the media. Whereas mind-expanding drugs were believed to open up new possibilities for personal development, the treatment of sex offenders and brainwashing were seen as a way to restrictively reprogramme people's minds, bodies and behaviour. Winston Smith's re-education in Part 3 of *Nineteen Eighty-Four* could also be considered a form of brainwashing (although the term had not yet been in use when Orwell wrote the novel).

Hence Burgess could draw both on Orwell's literary model and on public debates during the 1950s and early 1960s when devising the novel's 'Ludovico Technique', whose very name evoked Eastern European referents, as did the name of the man in charge of the treatment (Dr Brodsky).

Another form of Eastern European influence seems to be at work in the very language that the novel's teenagers use. Dr Branom characterises it as follows: 'most of the roots are Slav. Propaganda. Subliminal penetration' (p. 91). Using this slang, the novel's first-person narrator Alex looks back on his later teenage years (from ages fifteen to eighteen), which occur in an unnamed city in what is – from the perspective of 1962, when the novel was published – the near future. At the end of the novel (pp. 148–9), Alex's narration switches to present tense, which suggests that he is eighteen when he is writing down the story we read.[27] The novel is divided into three parts, each consisting of seven chapters and about fifty pages long in the Penguin edition (fifty-six, forty-one and forty-seven pages to be precise). The first chapter of each part, and also the final chapter of the book, starts with the question 'What's it going to be then, eh?', indicating that the issue of choice is central to the novel. Part 1 focuses on Alex's crimes and his arrest, Part 2 on his time in prison and his treatment, and Part 3 on his experiences after he is released, with Chapter 20 covering his time in hospital. Chapter 21 picks up the story a little while after Alex has left the hospital. He has a new gang and once again frequents the Korova Milk Bar, but he no longer engages in criminal activities. After meeting one of his former 'droogs', now married and working in insurance, Alex resolves to grow up and settle down as well, with a wife and child. The novel ends with the words: 'But you, O my brothers, remember sometimes thy little Alex that was. Amen. And all that cal [shit]' (p. 149).

Burgess was unsure about this final chapter, and, according to Andrew Biswell, his typescript of the novel dated August 1961 contains a handwritten note at the end of the penultimate chapter: 'Should we end here? An optional "epilogue" follows' (Biswell, 2005, p. 252). In fact, the question of where to end the novel was answered differently by his British and his American editors. Hence, the Heinemann edition published in the UK in May 1962 contained the final chapter, while it was dropped from the Norton edition published in the US early the following year. The implication of the British edition is that, given the opportunity, Alex eventually makes the right moral choice (although he feels no remorse for his previous behaviour and is sure that, in future, his own son will simply repeat his own delinquency). The implication of the American edition is that Alex will return to his former way of life so that the novel ends pretty much where it started (cp. Biswell, 2005, pp. 247–9). The final words of this edition describe Alex's response to hearing Beethoven's *Ninth Symphony* again:

> When it came to the Scherzo I could viddy myself very clear running and running on like very light and mysterious nogas [feet], carving the whole litso [face] of the creeching world with my cut-throat britva [razor]. And there was the slow movement and the lovely last singing movement still to come. I was cured all right. (p. 139)

Adaptation Projects

The very positive American reception of Burgess's novel (as discussed earlier) was partly due to the fact that, while it was set in another country, the story nevertheless resonated strongly with recent developments in the US. Crime rates had been rising dramatically since the mid-1950s, especially for violent crimes committed by juveniles (Gilbert, 1986, pp. 66–71; Schneider, 1999, pp. 74–7). By 1963, juvenile delinquency had been a topic of intense public debate for two decades. The debate, which involved politicians, social workers, educators, academics and cultural commentators of all stripes, had got started during the war in 1942–3 and had refused to go away afterwards (from 1953 onwards, a strong emphasis was placed on the alleged influence of media – especially films, comics and television – on juvenile delinquents).[28] At the same time, 'teenagers' had come to be recognised, and were widely discussed, as an important new force in the American economy and in American culture

(Palladino, 1996; Hine, 1999, Chs 12–13). All of this meant that *A Clockwork Orange* could be understood by its American reviewers as an intensely topical story, which helps to explain their enthusiasm for it. Yet there is also something inexplicable, indeed deeply disturbing about this enthusiasm, in particular the eagerness of several reviewers to welcome Alex's ability at the end of the novel to return to his old, violent ways, and to celebrate his crimes as acts of resistance against an oppressive political order, as an expression of his hunger for life.

The list of Alex's crimes is long: a brutal attack on a scholar in the streets, the robbing of a store, the beating-up of a drunk, a fight with a rival gang, the theft of a car, a home invasion culminating in a gang rape, vandalising a train carriage, an assault on his droogs, the murder of an old woman (all of these in Part 1) and the killing of a cellmate in prison (in Part 2). Perhaps the most shocking of all his deeds – acknowledged by one of the reviewers mentioned earlier who described Alex as a 'child-molesting teddy boy' (*Berkeley Gazette*, 1963) – is what he does to two girls 'who couldn't have been more than ten' (p. 36). After he picks them up in a record shop, he takes them to his room, gets them drunk and brutally rapes them, at the end of which they are 'all bruised' and 'going ow ow ow' (p. 39). There is no space here to explore how it is possible that Alex could be perceived as a kind of hero in the US. However it is worth noting that for any such exploration, Norman Mailer's highly influential 1957 essay 'The White Negro' would be an important reference point insofar as it celebrates 'the hipster [as] a philosophical psychopath' (p. 287), who resists the demands of a 'totalitarian society' (by which Mailer means the United States, p. 284) and forever searches, not least with acts of extreme violence (including sexual violence), for 'an orgasm more apocalyptic than the one which preceded it' (p. 291).[29] In his comments on psychopathology, Mailer gives pride of place to Robert Lindner's classic 1944 psychoanalytical study *Rebel without a Cause: The Story of a Criminal Psychopath*, which deals with an extraordinarily violent and precociously sexual juvenile delinquent and, since it mostly consists of transcriptions of therapy sessions, is largely rendered in his own words.[30] This study later provided the title – but not much else except for the shared concern with juvenile delinquency – for James Dean's most iconic movie, James Dean being, of course, one of post-war America's most celebrated hipsters (Mailer, 1957/1961, p. 282).[31] In this way, the most mainstream aspects of American culture were connected to a dark undercurrent of psychopathology, and to its veneration in American intellectual culture and elsewhere.

Perhaps this helps to explain Andy Warhol's interest in the novel, which Stephen Koch relates to the fact that he was 'fascinated by the tough male illiterate … the image of rough virility' (p. 69). Warhol acquired the film rights for $3,000 and in spring 1965 he produced an experimental movie entitled *Vinyl*, which Koch describes as 'a series of cinematic tableaux, a set of sexualised poses', involving beatings, torture, masochism and dancing among a group of men who are being observed by a glamorous woman (1991, p. 73; cp. Watson, 2003, pp. 199–203). While this *very* loose adaptation of Burgess's novel was never expected to reach a mainstream audience, it would initially appear to be quite surprising that soon afterwards attempts were made to turn *A Clockwork Orange* into a Hollywood movie. From the remorseless teenage criminal who goes unpunished in the end to the story's relentless violence, there were countless obstacles to producing a script that could have passed the restrictions of Hollywood's self-imposed Production Code.[32] The Code had been in place since the 1930s and was used by the Motion Picture Association of America (MPAA), the trade organisation of the major producers and distributors, to ensure that all films were, in principle, suitable for the whole family – because, unlike in other countries such as the UK, in the US there were no age classifications for movies.

However, times were changing. When the novelist and essayist Terry Southern (who had made his name in the film world by working on Kubrick's *Dr. Strangelove*), driven perhaps by a dark fascination with the novel's psychopathic hero and working through his lawyer and business manager Si Litvinoff, acquired an option on the film rights for *A Clockwork Orange* for $1,000 in spring 1966 (Hill, 2001, p. 149), the Production Code Adminstration (PCA) was still fully operational. Yet, by the time Southern and the British photographer Michael Cooper had completed the first draft of their script in August 1966 (Southern and Cooper, 1966), under a development deal with Paramount (Hill, 2001, p. 149), the end of the Code was in sight. Both the text of the Production Code and its implementation had already been undergoing a process of liberalisation since the end of World War II, and an increasing number of films had been released (mostly by small independent distributors) without the PCA's Seal of Approval.[33] Predictably, filmmakers as well as film critics and also, perhaps, certain audience segments and indeed studio executives, found the limitations that continued to be placed on what Hollywood films could show and how they could show it, far too strict. When Jack Valenti, who soon let it be known that he was no supporter of the Code, was appointed as the new head of the MPAA in April 1966, things began to move very fast (Valenti, 2007, Chs 10–11; Vaughn, 2006, pp. 16–26). A dispute erupted between Warner Bros. and the PCA about bad language in *Who's Afraid of Virginia Woolf?*; Valenti helped to settle it in June when the film was given a Seal of Approval, being exempted from certain Code stipulations under the condition that it was advertised with the warning 'No One under 18 Admitted without Parent', which in effect introduced an age classification.[34] In September 1966, Valenti revealed a new Production Code, which made age classification the new norm because films which transgressed the old Code's stipulations could now be released with the label 'Suggested for Mature Audiences' (Sandler, 2007, pp. 35–41). Soon the majority of films approved by the PCA carried this label (Leff and Simmons, 1990, p. 270).

In the light of these developments, Paramount's support for Southern and Cooper's *A Clockwork Orange* project becomes more understandable. In addition, it is worth considering other factors influencing the production decisions of the major studios during this period. The power of pressure groups such as the Catholic Legion of Decency was declining rapidly (Walsh, 1996, and Black, 1998), official film censorship by states and municipalities was disappearing (Wittern-Keller, 2008, Chs 10–12) and the interpretation and enforcement of obscenity laws was becoming much less rigorous

(McGeady, 1974; Heins, 2001, Ch. 3). All of this meant that Hollywood was now free to break long-standing taboos, and in the face of shrinking audiences this appeared to be a strategy worth trying out. Much like developments in the UK, in the US, cinema attendance levels had dropped catastrophically since their historical peak in 1943–4, with ticket sales in 1965 being less than a quarter of what they had been in 1944 (Finler, 2003, pp. 378–9). Ever since the 1940s, Hollywood had known that its main audience was composed of urban teenagers and young adults, and the importance of the youth audience had only increased during the 1950s and 1960s (Doherty, 1988, pp. 61–6; Krämer, 2005, pp. 59–60).[35] While Hollywood catered specifically to this demographic group with a range of films (cp. Doherty, 1988), its most expensive productions, and also its most successful releases both in the US and in the rest of the world, were historical epics and musicals addressed to an all-encompassing family audience. Intriguingly, at the beginning of 1966, *Variety*'s (not inflation-adjusted) all-time chart revealed that the third highest-grossing musical, and the tenth highest-grossing film of any genre, in American history featured juvenile gangs: *West Side Story* (1961) (*Variety*, 1966, p. 6). Also among the top forty all-time hits were a historical comedy-drama about the sexual adventures of a young English rake (*Tom Jones*, 1963) and a thriller about a youthful psychotic killer (*Psycho*, 1960). These precursors would seem to suggest that, if it was toned down sufficiently to avoid offending too many people, a film version of *A Clockwork Orange* might have considerable box-office potential. Many other high-profile film projects featuring copious amounts of explicit sex and/or graphic violence, or breaking other taboos (such as interracial marriage), were in production in 1966 – notably *Bonnie and Clyde*, *The Graduate* and *Guess Who's Coming to Dinner*, which were to become three of the next year's ten biggest hits as well as three of its five Best Picture nominees at the Academy Awards (Harris, 2009).

In these auspicious circumstances, the *Clockwork Orange* project gathered momentum. In April 1967, the *New York Times* reported that, working closely with Southern, Litvinoff, who had in the meantime set himself up as a film producer, was planning 'to film [*A Clockwork Orange*] independently in England next February' (*New York Times*, 1967; it is somewhat unclear what is meant by 'independent' here because the project was still backed by Paramount). The planned move to England was in line with Hollywood's heavy investments in the UK in the 1960s (cp. Dickinson and Street, 1985, pp. 233–40; and Murphy, 1992, Ch. 11). Production costs in the UK were lower than in California and, if enough British personnel were employed, a film shot in Britain also qualified for government subsidies. In addition, for decades Hollywood had produced a steady stream of films based on British source material and set in Britain, and across the post-war period, it had become increasingly obvious that such films could best be made in Britain, using British casts and locations (Stubbs, 2007). Last but not least, by the mid-1960s, Britain had become an important exporter of pop music and fashion, which created plenty of opportunities for linking film productions to such music and fashion. Indeed, at various points the names of both The Beatles and The Rolling Stones were associated with Southern and Litvinoff's *Clockwork Orange* project, as were British actors, such as David Hemmings, and British directors like John Boorman (*New York Times*, 1967; Ornstein, 1968; Hill, 2001, p. 149).

Nevertheless, Southern and Cooper's script was never produced. The files of the BBFC indicate what was probably the main reason. Southern and Cooper's script was submitted to the BBFC in May 1967, and although it removed much of the controversial material contained in the novel (notably the rape of the little girls), the BBFC wrote to the producers: 'we would not be able to pass the film. We consider that an unrelieved diet of hooliganism by teenagers is not only thoroughly undesirable but also dangerous' (BBFC, 1967). Even if the screenplay were to be revised substantially, with all 'cruelty and obscenity' removed in addition to all casual violence, it would remain problematic. For one thing, the censor noted, the teenage slang used in the script made it 'extremely difficult to read'. The letter ended with a warning to the film's studio backers: '[the film] is most unlikely to be shown in this country'. Britain was an important export market for Hollywood, and the BBFC's warning suggested that the adaptation of *A Clockwork Orange* would probably run into similar censorship problems in other countries as well. So it is not surprising that Paramount withdrew from the project at this time.

Only two years later the situation had changed quite dramatically. In the wake of the introduction of the 'suggested for mature audiences' label in the US, the box-office charts of 1967 came to be dominated by taboo-breaking films (Krämer, 2005, pp. 47–58, 106–7). In addition to the three already mentioned, the list of the year's ten top-grossing movies also included the extremely violent war movie *The Dirty Dozen* and the adaptation of Jacqueline Susann's sex-and-drugs bestseller *The Valley of the Dolls*. This trend was intensified by the introduction of the ratings system in autumn 1968.[36] Similar to procedures already in place in other countries (including the UK), each film was given a rating which indicated whether it was appropriate or not for young children and teenagers. Compared to other rating systems, however, Hollywood's approach was astonishingly liberal. For example, the second most restrictive category – 'R' – did not actually exclude children under sixteen, but merely required that they were accompanied by an adult. Only the most restrictive category – 'X' – excluded children altogether. It is important to note that the American 'X' was a kind of default category. If Hollywood's Code and Rating Administration (CARA) decided it could not give any other rating to a film, that film automatically received an 'X'. CARA could not refuse a certificate, which meant that, in principle, *anything* was possible now. By contrast, the BBFC, which had used a ratings system since it had been set up as a self-regulatory body by the film industry in 1912 and provided guidance for local authorities that were in charge of official censorship, regularly refused to certify films and thus in effect banned them in Britain. Furthermore, in many cases the BBFC handed out an 'X' rating only after having required extensive cuts.

Despite the freedom afforded by the new ratings system in the US, commercial considerations discouraged the major studios from investing heavily in films which could only ever get an 'X' rating, because that rating excluded what the film industry knew to be a key audience segment, namely young teenagers (thirteen to fifteen; this was made worse when CARA in March 1970 raised the age limit for both 'R' and 'X' from sixteen to seventeen; Steinberg, 1980, p. 402). Still, during the first twelve months of the operation of the new ratings system (from November 1968 to October 1969), the majors released sixteen 'X'-rated movies (p. 402). Among them was *Midnight Cowboy*, which featured, among many other things, male prostitution, homosexuality and drug abuse, and not only became the third highest-grossing film of 1969 in the US, but also won Academy Awards for Best Picture, Best Director and Best Adapted Screenplay (p. 243). Together with the astounding commercial and critical success of *Midnight Cowboy*, the performance of the drug-and-sex-fuelled road movie *Easy Rider* and the partner-swapping sex drama *Bob & Ted & Carol & Alice*, both of which made it into the US top ten of 1969, indicated that taboo-breaking was now big business for Hollywood, a trend which was confirmed in 1970 when two in places extremely brutal and gory films, which mixed violence with comedy, made it into the annual top ten (*M*A*S*H* and *Catch-22*).

Mirroring developments in the US, the BBFC also underwent a process of dramatic liberalisation in the late 1960s (although it would remain much more restrictive than CARA), and, like in the US, this was accompanied by the weakening of obscenity laws.[37] Such liberalisation facilitated the production of ever more explicitly sexual and graphically violent and otherwise taboo-breaking films in the UK, which, by the early 1970s, achieved major box-office success in this country (cp. Hunt, 1998, Chs 2–3 and 6–8), as did similarly transgressive films imported from the US. Indeed, when examining the end-of-year box-office reports for the UK in film-industry trade journals, *Kinematograph Weekly* and *Motion Picture Herald* (the reports being published every year in mid-December and at the beginning of January, respectively), we can note a dramatic change in hit patterns which parallels that in the US. From 1967 onwards, extremely violent films such as *Bonnie and Clyde*, *The Dirty Dozen*, *The Good, the Bad and the Ugly* (1966, UK release 1968), *M*A*S*H* and *Soldier Blue* (1970), as well as quite sexually explicit films such as *Barbarella* (1967), *The Graduate* (1967), *Candy* (1968), *Women in Love*

(1969), *Easy Rider* and *Midnight Cowboy* were among the top-grossing films of each year in the UK (Hall, 1999, vol. 2, p. 146).

These developments in the UK and the US from 1967 to 1970 provide the context for renewed attempts to turn Burgess's *A Clockwork Orange* into a British-made Hollywood movie. In January 1969, Litvinoff asked Anthony Burgess to adapt his own novel for a film to be directed by Nicolas Roeg (Biswell, 2005, pp. 337–8). Burgess substantially reworked the story of *A Clockwork Orange*, introducing some new material and leaving out other material, notably the twenty-first and final chapter of the British edition (Burgess, 1969). It is unclear why nothing came of the Burgess/Roeg version of *A Clockwork Orange* (apart from the fact that failure to get a production off the ground is the norm rather than the exception in the film industry). We do know, however, that, by February 1970, Litvinoff was corresponding with Stanley Kubrick and the press was announcing that Kubrick would adapt the novel himself.

Stanley Kubrick's Adaptation

On 3 February 1970, a headline in the film-industry trade paper *Variety* announced: 'Kubrick Will Make *Clockwork* for W[arner] B[rothers]' (*Variety*, 1970). The brief article described Burgess's novel as 'a black-comedy treatment of teenage violence in a futuristic welfare society'. On the same day, an article in the *New York Times* provided some background information. Kubrick was introduced as 'a 41-year-old New Yorker who has been living and working in England during the last few years' (Weiler, 1970). The new project was on a tight schedule. Kubrick, who was reported to be 'writing the screenplay' himself, planned to start shooting 'in London this summer'. Curiously, the article ended with a comment which suggested that *A Clockwork Orange* was a stop-gap measure caused by the delay of a much weightier film project: 'Once *A Clockwork Orange* is completed, Mr. Kubrick plans to return his attention to *Napoleon*, an epic-scale treatment of

Napoleon's career on which he has been working since July 1968.' In some ways, Kubrick's involvement with the *Clockwork Orange* project had run parallel to his work on his Napoleon biopic all along. Terry Southern had given the novel to Kubrick during the production of *2001: A Space Odyssey*, presumably to entice him to get involved in the project at that point (Houston, 1971/2001, p. 109). However, Kubrick chose the Napoleon film as his next project, and it is only when several attempts, in the course of 1969, to get studio funding for this big-budget epic came to nothing (cp. Castle, 2010, especially the volumes 'Text' and 'Production') that he finally read Burgess's novel and decided to adapt it. A few days after the press had announced Kubrick's new project on 3 February 1970, Si Litvinoff sent him a letter which indicates that Kubrick had not in fact signed any contract yet (Litvinoff, 1970). However, he probably did so soon thereafter because by mid-February he was working hard on the *Clockwork Orange* script. Kubrick had completed a first draft of the screenplay by 28 February 1970 (Kubrick, 1970a).

The filmmaker's fairly sudden decision to adapt *A Clockwork Orange* in February 1970 needs to be seen against the backdrop of his work during the preceding decade. With the massive box-office hit *Spartacus* (1960), Kubrick had established himself as one of Hollywood's leading directors (after a commercially rather undistinguished career in the 1950s; Sklar, 1988, pp. 115–17). He then joined the exodus of Hollywood producers to England, where he would make three critically acclaimed and commercially successful films in the 1960s (cp. Sklar, 1988, pp. 117–19; Krämer, 2010b, pp. 32–3, 90–3). Working with a largely British crew, he shot *Lolita* (1962) at Elstree Studios in 1961–2, with post-production also taking place in the UK (LoBrutto, 1998, pp. 202–3, 212–14). On *Lolita*, he cast British stars Peter Sellers and James Mason, and his collaboration with Sellers continued when he returned to England for *Dr. Strangelove* (1964) (pp. 235–43). This film was based on a novel by a British writer, Peter George's *Two Hours to Doom* (1958, published under the title *Red Alert* in the US). Kubrick worked closely with George on the film's script, and he developed his next film, *2001: A Space Odyssey*, in close collaboration with British author Arthur C. Clarke (Krämer,

2010b). Once again the film's production and post-production took place in England from summer 1965 onwards, and during this time Kubrick and his family moved there permanently (LoBrutto, 1998, p. 319). In this context, Kubrick's decision in 1970 finally to produce a film which was not only based on the work of a British author and made in the UK with a British crew and British actors, but was also set in England, making use of a wide range of locations there, has a certain logic to it.

By 1970, Kubrick had also started expressing doubts about his adaptation of Vladimir Nabokov's scandalous 1955 bestseller *Lolita* about a middle-aged man's sexual obsession, and sexual relations, with a twelve-year-old girl:

> [B]ecause of all the pressure of the Production Code and the Catholic Legion of Decency at the time, I believe I didn't sufficiently dramatize the erotic aspect of Humbert's relationship with Lolita. ... If I could do the film over again, I would have stressed the erotic component of their relationship with the same weight Nabokov did. (Gelmis, 1970/2001, pp. 87–8)

Nabokov's book consists largely of a first-person narrative in which Humbert, employing a very distinctive style and only at the very end displaying a sense of guilt and remorse, relates his obsessions and adventures, including scenes in which he drugs, bullies and rapes a young girl. These similarities with Burgess's novel suggest that its adaptation – after the demise of the Production Code and the Legion of Decency – offered Kubrick an opportunity to explore male sexuality and violence in a more explicit fashion than he had been able to do with his adaptation of *Lolita*. Yet, despite all the nudity, sexual acts and sexual violence in Kubrick's film, he shied away from staging the two attacks on little girls narrated in the novel (the second one has Billyboy and his gang tormenting a girl 'not more than ten' when interrupted by Alex and his droogs; Burgess, 1962/1972, p. 16). Kubrick explained that, among other things, the age of his actors, and hence of the characters they played, had been a problem, as well as the deeply disturbing nature of the act itself: 'In the book Alex is fifteen. We really don't want to see fifteen-year-olds abusing ten-year-old girls, but that is still a very different matter from a twenty-five-year-old man abusing ten-year-old girls' (Siskel, 1972/2001, p. 123).

In addition to his regrets about *Lolita*, Kubrick had further reasons for welcoming the lifting of restrictions on Hollywood filmmakers, because ever since the 1950s he had consistently pursued projects (mostly adaptations of novels) which explored all aspects of human sexuality, and, more often than not, the PCA had found these projects unacceptable so that the films could not get made.[38] In the late 1960s and early 1970s, Kubrick seemed determined to make up for lost time: his Napoleon script highlighted the protagonist's sex life in a very explicit manner (Kubrick, 1969/2010; cp. Gelmis, 1970/2001, p. 84), and he expressed an interest in adapting Arthur Schnitzler's erotic novella *Traumnovelle*, which would much later become his final film, *Eyes Wide Shut* (1999) (LoBrutto, 1998, p. 329; *LA Herald Examiner*, 1971). Most intriguingly, in the mid-1960s, after the completion of *Dr. Strangelove*, on which they had worked together, Kubrick and Terry Southern discussed the idea of a major Hollywood director making a big-budget hardcore porn movie (Hill, 2001, pp. 121–2). This became the basis for Southern's (quite pornographic) novel *Blue Movie* (1970), the dedication of which reads: 'for the great Stanley K'. While Kubrick was sent drafts of Southern's novel (the cover page stating: 'based on a story by Stanley Kubrick') at the end of 1969 and the beginning of 1970, it is unlikely that he seriously considered turning it into a movie.[39] Nevertheless, this project indicates that writers and directors like Southern and Kubrick were willing to consider the extremes to which Hollywood filmmaking might be taken after external restrictions had been removed, and, of course, *A Clockwork Orange* turned out to be the perfect manifestation of venturing to such extremes.

Unfortunately, in sharp contrast to the numerous interviews Kubrick gave about the film in the run-up to, and during, its release (see my discussion of these in Part 1), the countless documents in the filmmaker's archive contain hardly any direct comments on his approach to, and his intentions for, the film's production. In one of the few exceptions to this rule, Kubrick explained the work he had done on the script, presumably so as to clarify that the film was indeed based on his script rather than on those written by Southern and Cooper and by Burgess. His 'memorandum' starts: 'I have taken nothing from any of the other screenplays. All the screenplays have substantially followed the plot of the novel' (Kubrick, 1971). He then listed 'significant innovations which do not appear in any previous screenplay drafts or in the original novel. This list does not include changes of detail, staging, location or dialogue.' It *does* include 'Alex doing a little tap dance' while performing 'Singin' in the Rain', which 'will serve later on as the means of F. Alexander identifying Alex'. The Catlady has been transformed from 'an old, eccentric woman with a walking stick' into a 'youngish, diet-slim 40-year-old, in a room full of pornographic art and sculpture'. Her 'phone call to the Police Station explains how it is that the police arrive at the end of the scene'. The '[p]rison check-in … is an innovation', as is 'the means by which Alex attracts the Governor's attention' and the transfer to the Ludovico medical facility. The encounter with the drunk on the riverbank replaces Alex's encounter in the novel with another of his victims in a library: 'It is now more plausible that the police arrive at the spur of the moment.' Mr Alexander's live-in helper, Julian, is an addition; whereas '[i]n other versions of the scene it was not clear why Alex didn't leave' Mr Alexander's house, '[t]he presence of Julian … solves this problem'. Mr Alexander's 'call to the other two radical conspirators … helps to explain what is going on with more clarity'. The new dialogue between the female conspirator and Alex about his response to Beethoven's *Ninth Symphony* after the Ludovico treatment 'helps clarify' this crucial matter, and the way in which the next scene is shot makes explicit 'what the conspirators are actually up to' when they drive Alex to a suicide attempt, which is 'something that has to be inferred in other versions'.

Perhaps quite surprisingly, Kubrick here mostly discusses formal issues to do with establishing, clarifying or highlighting causal links between events in the story, where previously such links had been missing, unclear or implied.

This is reminiscent of some of the interview statements quoted in Part 1, in which Kubrick insists that he is primarily interested in stories as formal constructs, rather than as vehicles for themes and ideas – although it is probably understood that a well-constructed story will serve more effectively for the development of themes and the communication of ideas as well. Still, there is, in Kubrick's statements, a basic disjunction between the clarity he is obviously striving for at the level of the story (what happens, how and why?) and the variable meanings and pleasures audiences are encouraged to take from the film (how does it feel, what does it mean?). With this in mind, let's take another look at the film's ending and how it emerges from the script-development process.

Early on in the scriptwriting process, Kubrick must have looked at the two previous attempts to adapt Burgess's novel; his personal collection contains annotated versions of both Southern and Cooper's 1966 script and Burgess's 1969 script. However, as noted in Kubrick's memorandum, there is no discernible influence of these scripts on his work – with one notable exception. Burgess's decision to drop the contents of the novel's twenty-first chapter from his script must have stood out to Kubrick, and also Southern and Cooper's indecisiveness about the ending. Their script has two conclusions (the second labelled 'alternative ending'): number one is a scene showing Alex in the hospital being able once again to enjoy depictions of violence; number two is a scene in which Alex, having left the hospital, contemplates settling down (Southern and Cooper, 1966). After a decade of indecision about the ending of Burgess's novel (Kubrick had copies of both the British and the American edition), he may have taken the lead from the author's last statement on the matter, which was to drop the conclusion of the British edition from his own script. Kubrick's screenplay of 28 February 1970 ends with Alex in the hospital (Kubrick, 1970a). He has violent fantasies, including what the script calls a 'rape fantasy' (with people standing by and clapping), before the Minister of the Interior visits him. After Alex has come to an agreement with the minister, he listens to Beethoven's *Ninth Symphony* on his own. The script does not indicate that he is having any further visions at this point. Instead Alex's voiceover simply speaks the only slightly modified final sentences of Chapter 20 of the novel (quoted above), which evoke an image of him running around with a sharp razor, slashing at the world. Kubrick's 'Shooting Script' of 7 September 1970 ends in the same way (Kubrick, 1970b).

While the scripts thus imply that Alex returns to violence at the end (initially in his fantasy and then, most probably, in reality), the film ends very differently, as we saw in Part 2. It is very open to different responses and raises the possibility that Alex has changed, because his sexual fantasy appears to be much more about pleasure (for both sexes) than about Alex's violent domination of a woman. And yet, it is apparently very difficult for viewers to keep an open mind about the ending, to see the possibility of redemption. After Kubrick had completed the film, Mai Harris, a staff member transcribed it shot by shot; the entry for the very last shot reads as follows:

> RAPE FANTASY – SLOW MOTION
> MS ALEX and GIRL romping about naked in polystyrene.
> PEOPLE standing L. and R. of them.
> 'I was cured all right.' (Harris, 1972)

One might say that, going against the American edition of the novel and against his own scripts, with the film's actual ending, Kubrick was striving to maximise ambiguity (as he had so clearly done with *2001: A Space Odyssey*) – but, judging by the response of Mai Harris and indeed of many reviewers and academic critics, on this occasion Kubrick's striving for ambiguity seems to have failed.

Conclusion

When Anthony Burgess wrote *A Clockwork Orange* in 1961, he drew on two classics of British dystopian fiction – *Brave New World* and *Nineteen Eighty-Four*

– while also engaging with key developments in post-war Britain such as the emergence of so-called 'teenagers', rising crime rates, debates about Americanisation and anxieties about 'Teddy Boys', media effects and brainwashing. In the US, Burgess's novel was widely perceived as a compelling and horrifying account not only of future developments but also of the present state of British and, to a lesser extent, American society. Against the backdrop of its dystopian political vision, the actions of its psychopathic protagonist, who commits terrible crimes without any sense of guilt or remorse and without any empathy for his victims' suffering, exerted a dark attraction for many reviewers and also for filmmakers. Dramatic changes in American (and also in British) film culture across the 1950s and 1960s – notably the shrinking of cinema audiences and the increasing dominance of young cinemagoers as well as the lifting of external and internal restrictions on what mainstream films could show – made it possible, and commercially attractive, to consider a Hollywood adaptation of *A Clockwork Orange* from 1966 onwards (after Andy Warhol's underground version of 1965). Hollywood at this point was an industry almost as active in the UK as it was in the US, and from the outset the intention was to produce the Hollywood version of *A Clockwork Orange* in a British studio with a British cast and crew.

It was understood that, despite the liberalisation of film-industry self-regulation, official censorship and obscenity legislation, certain elements of the novel would have to be toned down (notably the sexual attacks on little girls) so as to avoid offending too many people, and that, even if such toning down occurred, the film would encounter much resistance, as indeed it did when Terry Southern and Michael Cooper's script was rejected by the BBFC in 1967. Nevertheless, the extraordinary output of taboo-breaking films, and their huge commercial impact in both the US and the UK, from 1967 onwards reduced resistance to the *Clockwork Orange* project, and also prepared the ground for its later success. By the time Stanley Kubrick got involved, he had an enviable track record of four commercial and critical hits in a row, and no doubt he meant for *A Clockwork Orange* to extend this winning streak. The project also gave him the chance to explore sexuality in a more direct and explicit fashion than he had been able to do before, with several of his previous attempts in this direction having been thwarted by the Production Code Administration. Largely disregarding earlier attempts to adapt the novel, Kubrick's version returned to the source text, yet he followed Burgess's own script as well as the American edition of the novel when he excluded the material covered in the twenty-first chapter. It appears that during the film's production, Kubrick was primarily concerned with streamlining and tightening up the story and then to stage, shoot and edit the story so as to make it 'interesting' (see Part 1). Kubrick seemed to have been confident that the themes and ideas developed in the novel he was adapting would shine through powerfully once they were presented in such an interesting filmic manner, but he also designed the film's ending so as to maximise the story's potential meanings and the variety of ways in which audiences might respond to it. At the same time, both at the script stage and after the film's completion when a staff member had to transcribe the finished product, the impression that Alex was first and foremost a violent sexual predator was so overpowering that the film's ending, in principle open to different readings, was consistently interpreted as Alex's return to his old ways. Hence, the final shot of the story, which could be seen as a redemptive fantasy of socially approved and mutually satisfying sexual intercourse, was most likely to be understood as 'rape'. Indeed, as we will see in Part 4, this understanding underpinned much of the film's provocative marketing and controversial reception.

 **PART 4**

MARKETING AND RECEPTION

Introduction

A Clockwork Orange was released by Warner Bros. in the United States on 19 December 1971, being shown initially in only four cities (*Variety*, 1971). Such a restricted release shortly before the end of the year was typical for high-profile films at the time, because it meant that they were fresh in people's minds when various lists for the best films of the year and the nominations for major awards were decided upon shortly afterwards. If a film was successful with critics and industry peers, its selection as the best, or one of the best, films of the year could then be used in the film's advertising when it was released to a larger number of movie theatres across the country – which is exactly what happened with *A Clockwork Orange*. Within a few weeks of its release, the film was named 'Best Motion Picture' of 1971 by the New York Film Critics' Association, and Kubrick won in the category 'Best Direction' (Steinberg, 1980, p. 269). The film was also listed as one of the year's ten best movies by the *New York Times* and *Time* magazine, and it was nominated for four Academy Awards, including Best Picture, Director and Adapted Screenplay (Steinberg, 1980, pp. 175, 179, 246). However, the critical reception of *A Clockwork Orange* was by no means unanimously positive; quite the contrary, its celebration in some quarters provoked vigorous responses. For example, *A Clockwork Orange* featured prominently in the *Harvard Lampoon*'s long-running 'Movie Worsts' awards. It headed the list of the year's 'Ten Worst Movies', while 'the entire Society of New York Film Critics' won the award intended to identify 'the film critic whose writing has most consistently explored the limits of bad taste' for naming *A Clockwork Orange* the best film of the year (Steinberg, 1980, p. 330).

It is probable that the accusation of bad taste was not only provoked by the content and style of the film itself, but also by its marketing. The press book issued by Warner Bros. at the beginning of 1972 displays the range of pictures and texts to be used in advertisements and on posters for the film. The film's shocking tagline stands out: 'Being the adventures of a young man whose principal interests are rape, ultra-violence and Beethoven' (Warner Bros., 1972). This is reminiscent of the initial tagline for Warner Bros.' groundbreaking and highly controversial 1967 hit, *Bonnie and Clyde*: 'They're young … they're in love … and they kill people' (Hoberman, 1998).[40] *Bonnie and Clyde* is a graphically violent and in places very funny drama about a pair of stylish, yet sexually dysfunctional Depression-era bankrobbers, which was widely regarded even at the time of its release as the beginning of a 'renaissance' in Hollywood cinema, the point of departure for a 'New Hollywood', but also as the moment when sex and violence and taboo-breaking of any kind took over mainstream movie theatres so that they were no longer places where the majority of the population, especially older people and children, would feel comfortable and safe (Krämer, 2005, pp. 1–66). Indeed, an increasing number of Americans stopped going to the movies altogether so that, by the time *A Clockwork Orange* was released, the cinema audience was smaller, and more narrowly focused on educated, urban youth, than ever before – or since (pp. 58–62). What is more, Hollywood was widely perceived at the time to be catering primarily to males, while largely ignoring the preferences, sensitivities and objections of female cinemagoers (Krämer, 1999, pp. 95–7). Thus, the focus of *A Clockwork Orange*'s tagline on a 'young man' mirrored precisely the group that could still be expected to go to the movies, and one might even see the reference to Beethoven as a nod to its comparatively high level of education. Indeed, the remainder of the press book, which included a lot of advice to cinema managers on how to attract audiences, on several occasions refers to 'music critics' and 'classical music … stations', 'the college and underground press' as well as 'college-operated radio stations', 'young people in college cinema and drama classes', 'film buffs' and 'cinema students', 'college students and other sophisticated moviegoers' (Warner Bros., 1972).

What exactly did the film's marketing offer to these educated young moviegoers, and notably the males among them? There were lots of assurances in ads and on posters that they would be seeing a critically approved film, a movie masterpiece, a work of art. References to the awards from the New York Film Critics' Association ('Best Picture', 'Best Director') and quotations from reviews were common: 'one of the few perfect movies I have seen in my lifetime' (Red Reed, *New York Sunday News*), 'a *tour de force* of extraordinary images, music, words and feeling' (Vincent Canby, *New York Times*), '[t]he kind of *tour de force* of the intellect and imagination that marks Kubrick as a true genius of the cinema' (Paul D. Zimmerman, *Newsweek*), 'so inventive and powerful that [it] can be viewed again and again and each time yield up fresh illuminations' (*Time*) (Warner Bros., 1972). So as to counter early criticisms of the film's disturbing violence and powerful visceral impact (as discussed at the beginning of Part 2), some of the ads included the following quotation: 'The much discussed violence? Don't worry about it ... do not be put off by all the hoo-ha. Go along and see it – it really is wild' (Susie Eisenhuth, *The Australian Sunday Telegraph*).

For people critical of the film, seeing such ads and posters cannot have been very reassuring. Audiences were basically invited to have a 'wild' time with the film's mixture of 'rape, ultra-violence and Beethoven', accompanying Alex in his 'adventures'. In addition, the paintings supporting the text were provocative, to say the least. From within the enlarged 'A' of the film's title, Alex, with his false eyelashes, bowler hat and an eyeball on his sleeves, stares at the viewers, pushing a knife towards them, apparently breaking through the very paper on which the ad or poster is printed so as to reach out into their reality. On posters, this image was often complemented by the figure of an almost naked woman leaning forward suggestively, whereby this figure was inserted in the space under Alex's fake eyeball and knife (fig. 24), indicating perhaps that she or women like her were the victims of Alex's ultra-violence. In this way, the implied threat of Alex reaching out to viewers with the knife in his hand is specifically associated with female targets, which once again would appear to be an invitation to male viewers to join Alex in his (sexually) violent endeavours. However, other posters and ads took a different approach. One poster used four stills from the film (including one from the attack on

24

the Alexanders) with the text: 'Being the adventures of a young man ... who loved a bit of the old ultra-violence ... went to jail, was brainwashed ... and came out cured ... or was he?' This statement not only outlines the film's story but also begins to address the questions it raises about totalitarian tendencies in contemporary society and about the morality of 'brainwashing'. In the press book's 'advertising supplement', which may well have been addressed specifically to the British market, an ad, using the tagline 'The Film Shocker to End Them All', asked: 'Are we headed for an ultra-violent society where sex and terror gangs rule the streets, and where law-and-order becomes the most important political issue?' Here the film's relevance for thinking about crime and the threats to law and order in contemporary society is foregrounded. If there is an invitation implied in this question, it is not to join the gangs, but to feel threatened by them and to work towards measures which might contain them.

In this part, I examine the success of the film and of its marketing campaign in the US and the UK, while also detailing the critical attacks *A Clockwork Orange* provoked, and the ways in which it got drawn into debates about the state of contemporary cinema and of contemporary society. The first section looks at the film's box-office performance in the US as well as the UK release pattern and its critical acclaim and commercial success there. The second section examines the debate about the film in the US with a particular emphasis on the implications of its 'X' rating. In the third section, I outline the scope and development of the debate about *A Clockwork Orange* in the UK, with a particular emphasis on fears and claims about copycat crimes.

Commercial and Critical Success

On 23 March 1972, the American trade press reported that *A Clockwork Orange* had been doing extremely well in the twenty-eight cinemas in which it had been shown in the US so far, having already earned $2.4 million in rentals (*Hollywood Reporter*, 1972). The film was scheduled to appear in fifty cinemas in April and to go on '[n]ational release' by appearing in hundreds of cinemas in cities and towns all over the US during the summer. The film had initially been released with an 'X' rating but Kubrick later submitted a slightly modified version of the film – with thirty seconds of material in the orgy scene and the gang-rape shown during the Ludovico treatment being replaced with less explicit takes – to CARA and on 22 August 1972, *A Clockwork Orange* received an 'R' (CARA, 1972; *Daily Variety*, 1972). According to CARA rules, the 'X'-rated version had to be withdrawn for sixty days before the new version could be released, which means that the film temporarily disappeared from American movie theatres. Upon its return, it continued to perform well, now being able to reach a wider audience, including younger teenagers and people, who in principle did not attend 'X'-rated movies. By the end of 1972, the film had grossed $12 million with another $1.5 million being added in 1973 and about half a million dollars in each of the next few years (see *Variety*'s 'All-Time Film Rental Champs', published in an early January issue every year). By the end of its extremely long run in American theatres, it had earned $17 million in rentals, which made it the seventh highest-grossing title among the 432 films released in the US in 1971 (Krämer, 2005, p. 108; Steinberg, 1980, p. 43).

The film's performance in the UK was equally impressive, combining early success with durability, although, right from the beginning, we can observe strong concerns about the film's possible impact on audiences. On 19 January 1972, a headline in *Variety* announced: 'Bouquets and Brickbats for Kubrick's *Orange* from British Critics' (*Variety*, 1972). The article noted that, with one exception, all the major newspapers had reviewed the film, which had been released in the UK on 13 January, very positively (cp. Barr, 1972). However, the one exception, the *Daily Telegraph*, had received support from 'the official Police Federation publication' which complained about the film's 'outstanding hideousness' (*Variety*, 1972; cp. Burden, 1972). A year later, the London *Times* reported that *A Clockwork Orange* was still playing in the Warner West End Theatre where it had originally opened on 13 January 1972 (*The Times*, 1973). In fact, until September 1972, the film had *only* been shown at that one movie theatre; it was then released in thirteen more cinemas across London, and from January 1973 in cinemas across the country (Allardyce-Hampshire, 1972, and Warner Bros., 1973). Of all films on limited release in 1972, only *The Godfather* had done better at the box office than *A Clockwork Orange* (*Films and Filming*, 1973). In January 1974, *Variety* announced that the film, which was still running at the Warner West End, had been the third highest-grossing film on general release in the UK in 1973, after *Live and Let Die* and *The Godfather* (*Variety*, 1974). The press noted that the initial focus on just one cinema and the belated rollout across London and then across the country was unusual. Indeed, the film's British distributor (Columbia/Warner) and the ABC cinema chain had planned a different release pattern but Kubrick had insisted on a very limited initial release (Karlin, 1972). According to an internal Warner Bros. memo of February 1972, Kubrick 'was, and is, afraid that the controversy which is going on over this film is dangerous and could lead to banning of the film' if it was widely shown (the film was indeed banned by various local authorities during its national release in 1973).[41]

When the end-of-year critical overviews for 1972 and 1973 were published, *A Clockwork Orange* was mentioned frequently. Both Alexander Walker of the *Evening Standard* and Derek Malcolm of the *Guardian* declared *A Clockwork Orange* the best film of 1972 (Walker, 1972; Malcolm, 1972). Even the *Daily Telegraph*, which had initially been critical of the film, now listed it as one of the ten best films of 1972, pointing out that it was probably the '[m]ost accomplished' British movie of the year (Gibbs, 1972). In a survey of a range of critics conducted by *Films Illustrated*, *A Clockwork Orange* came out on top as the best film of 1972, while it was ranked sixth in a poll of the magazine's readers (*Films Illustrated*, 1973). Similarly, a Gallup poll asking respondents about 'the best film you have seen in 1973' ranked *A Clockwork Orange* fourth (*Daily Telegraph*, 1973). In a February 1974 poll for *Disc* magazine, *A Clockwork Orange* came in at number three (*Disc*, 1974), and in the *Glasgow Herald*'s critical survey of the previous year's films in January 1974, *A Clockwork Orange* once again came out on top (Plowright, 1974).

Importantly, both the *Glasgow Herald* critic and, thirteen months earlier, David Robinson of the *Financial Times* praised *A Clockwork Orange* precisely because of the controversy surrounding it. According to Robinson, in 1972 it had 'caused deep consternation at a moment when the "backlash" against the mood of permissiveness seemed to be gaining vigour' (Robinson, 1972). And in the *Glasgow Herald*, Molly Plowright reflected on the personal attacks she had suffered from readers and colleagues disagreeing with her praise of *A Clockwork Orange* in 1973. She understood the film as 'a dreadful warning': 'the thugs and muggers of today are inviting an even more horrifying reprisal from society in the future' (Plowright, 1974). Indeed, as demonstrated by the reports about the home invasion and sexual assault in Riverdale, New York, which I discussed in the Introduction, the existence of real-life 'thugs and muggers' had been central to the film's reception from the very beginning. However, while real-life crimes came to dominate the debate about *A Clockwork Orange* in the UK, they only played a minor role in the film's American reception.

The US Controversy

Apart from the release date and the artwork and text used in ads and posters, the key decision in presenting *A Clockwork Orange* to the public was to go with the 'X' rating given to the film by the Code and Rating Administration, rather than re-editing it in order to get an 'R' for the initial release (as noted earlier, such re-editing only took place later in 1972). *Variety* suggested that accepting the 'X' may have been Kubrick's decision, rather than that of the studio financing and distributing the film: 'Kubrick is thought to have had final cut rights on *Clockwork* so WB couldn't have battled the rating if it wanted to' (*Variety*, 1971). Irrespective of Kubrick's contractual power, however, the *Variety* article implied that the film's distributor was quite willing to accept the 'X' rating: 'Warners is the only major [studio] to have two X features this year, with most of the other companies doing their utmost to avoid the rating.'[42] Indeed, during the twelve months from November 1970 to October 1971, only three out of 238 films submitted to CARA by the major studios and the leading 'minors' had been rated 'X', that is only about 1% of their overall output; this was down from 4% in the preceding two years (Steinberg, 1980, p. 402). For the twelve months from November 1971 to October 1972, only one film submitted by the majors and leading minors received an 'X'. This was *A Clockwork Orange*, for which CARA issued a certificate on 15 December 1971, only four days before the film's release (CARA, 1971).

Variety was apprehensive about the rating's commercial implications: 'The X-tag is known to cut into the number of dates a film can play in the US, though what that means to ultimate box office is difficult to determine' (*Variety*, 1971). Indeed, up to 50% of exhibitors in the US said that they would refuse to show 'X'-rated movies (according to a 1969 poll cited in Farber, 1972, p. 48; cp. Farber and Changas, 1972, cited in Wyatt, 2000, p. 244). Thus, the 'X' rating was very divisive, separating theatres willing to show films with this rating from those that did not show them. A survey conducted in July 1973 suggested that cinema audiences were similarly divided (although we have to be careful about projecting these results back to the early months of the release of *A Clockwork Orange*; by July 1973, 'X' had become more closely associated with hardcore pornography; cp. Wyatt, 2000). When a representative sample of people eighteen and older were asked about their 'least preferred type of movie', the category 'X rated' received far more votes than any other (34% of the total; the second most-prominent category was 'Horror/Monster' with 23%) (Newspaper Advertising Bureau, 1974). Not surprisingly, women objected to 'X'-rated films more strongly than men did; 45% listed them as their least favourite film type. Quite astonishingly, 10% of male respondents declared 'X'-rated films to be their 'most preferred type of movie'.[43] It would seem, then, that the 'X' rating set both movie theatres and audience segments against each other, notably men against women.

In many ways, the marketing campaign for *A Clockwork Orange* intensified the divisiveness of its rating. Complementing the provocative ads and posters discussed earlier, the theatrical trailer consisted of a rapid montage of extremely brief shots, in some cases consisting of only a few frames. It intercuts action taken from the film, containing plenty of violence, with sexual imagery taken from poster art and words flashing on the screen. Many of these words – such as 'witty', 'comic', 'exciting', 'thrilling' – suggested that the film would be a lot of fun, which one might find to be ironic, provocative or simply offensive. By March 1972, this provocative marketing, together with a large amount of extremely hostile press commentary on the film, resulted in the *Detroit News* taking a drastic measure. Responding specifically to the release of *A Clockwork Orange*, the paper announced in a widely publicised editorial on 19 March that from 26 March it 'no longer will publish display advertising [for] – or give editorial publicity to – X-rated motion pictures and those other unrated pictures, which, in our judgment, are of a pornographic nature'.[44] Among other things, this meant that the paper would no longer review 'X'-rated films. By this time, about thirty American newspapers had a similar policy regarding films rated 'X' by CARA, considering them all as equivalent to hardcore pornography or 'sadistic violence', which they felt should in no way be supported (*New York Times*, 1972). At a time when print advertising for movies, together with the free publicity provided by articles in newspapers and magazines, was much more important than brief trailers or film programmes shown on television (and also, probably, more important than poster displays, radio ads and theatrical trailers), this was a serious restriction. However, most of the thirty papers mentioned above probably continued, as the *Detroit News* said it would, to offer minimal information about 'X'-rated films in their movie listings, and also to report on '[g]eneral news developments concerning such pictures'; indeed, on 9 April 1972, the *Detroit News* printed a letter from Stanley Kubrick which attacked the paper's policy and also offered a defence of *A Clockwork Orange* (*New York Times*, 1972). Thus, an 'X'-rated film like *A Clockwork Orange* would have neither ads nor reviews or puff pieces in many newspapers, yet if it was controversial enough or made the news in any other way, these papers would still have to report on it.

The film's many supporters objected to the 'X' rating (e.g. Murphy, 1971; Reed, 1971) and to any actions against 'X'-rated films such as the one taken by the *Detroit News*, because they restricted access to what was considered an important film. The film's detractors also questioned the film's rating, often as part of a broad critique of the state of Hollywood and its place in American society. The *Christian Science Monitor* described *A Clockwork Orange* as 'a film so repellent its "X" rating seems not warning enough' (*Christian Science Monitor*, 1971). Clayton Riley's attack on the film in the *New York Times* covered all angles by describing the film as 'a monumental bore, a fitful parade of those technical bonbons that characterize our television commercials' (Riley, 1972). He then laid into its supporters among critics and audiences, who, he wrote, 'delight in deciphering [art], as if by doing so they became the possessor of some mystical insight, some delicious new registration of depravity'. This, for him, was not just a matter of bad taste and pretentiousness. With reference to Charles Manson, My Lai and Nazi terror, Riley objected to what he regarded as the film's central idea: 'the will to perpetrate evil is better than no will at all'. What is more, he feared that the film might actually inspire real-life violence: 'Enough brutality of an instructive nature is contained in *Orange* to provide a manual for the needs of every street gang and knuckle society in the US.' Interestingly, this anxiety was shared by Vincent Canby, whose second glowing review of the film was printed opposite Riley's article: 'there may be a very real problem when ... such stylized representations [of violence] are seen by immature audiences'.[45] Canby raised the possibility that the film might traumatise audiences or even move them to engage in violence themselves, which also appeared to be a concern of Riley's. However, this possibility was not explored much further in the American press. Instead, more general concerns about social disintegration and the political order became central to the debate.

In a comprehensive critique of the film in the *Village Voice*, Andrew Sarris pointed, like many other critics, to the attractiveness of its protagonist and to what, in his eyes, amounted to the film's apologetic account of his deeds: 'Alex and his friends are let off the hook. Anything this particular society gets, it asks for in the vile literalism of its lewdness' (Sarris, 1971; cp. Staiger, 2003, pp. 48–9). Then, in an ambiguous statement apparently referencing depictions of violence in other films and elsewhere in popular culture as well as real-life violence, Sarris turned apocalyptic: 'What frightens me is the chaos that engulfs us all. I am tired of the cult of violence. I am tired of people smashing other people and things in the name of freedom and self-expression.' This would appear to raise the spectre of the film's violence spilling over into the auditorium and into the streets, while also giving expression to Sarris's very negative view of where American culture and society were currently heading.

After the initial reviews, which mostly concentrated on this one film, had come out, *A Clockwork Orange* proceeded to become the focus of more general attacks on Hollywood and what were perceived to be troubling tendencies in American culture. Most notably, in February 1972, Fred M. Hechinger attacked *A Clockwork Orange* in an article entitled 'A Liberal Fights Back' in the *New York Times* as a film which promoted 'the thesis that man is irretrievably bad and corrupt', an idea he considered to be the very 'essence of fascism' (Hechinger, 1972). He argued that only 'the repressive, illiberal, distrustful, violent institutions of fascism' could 'be built on that pessimistic view of man's nature'. For Hechinger, *A Clockwork Orange* was only the most egregious example of a widespread trend in Hollywood, which was rooted in the 'deeply anti-liberal totalitarian nihilism emanating from beneath the counter-culture' that the studios had previously courted with a series of 'mindless youth-culture exploitation' films. According to Hechinger, these filmic trends had strong political implications: 'It is precisely because Hollywood's antennae have in the past been so sensitive in picking up the national mood that the anti-liberal trend' should be taken seriously as an indication of a fascist disposition in American society.[46] The following month saw another high-profile statement about *A Clockwork Orange* and the perceived crisis in American culture, this time from what appeared to be a very different political direction. Contradicting a positive review of the film in his own paper, the features editor of the *Pittsburgh Press* wrote on 20 March 1972, only one day after the dramatic announcement by the *Detroit Press* about its ban on advertising and publicity for 'X'-rated movies: 'If *Clockwork Orange* is the best movie of 1971, the whole motion picture industry is so sick, the ailment may be fatal. ... It is enough to make you throw up, morally and physically' (Allen, 1972; quoted in Litman, 1972).

Despite these formidable attacks on the film, and despite the limited number of cinemas in which it was shown and the restricted number of newspapers in which it was advertised, *A Clockwork Orange* was, as we have seen, enormously successful at the box office. An audience survey conducted early in the film's release, presumably by handing out a questionnaire after a regular screening of *A Clockwork Orange*, indicates the reasons for the film's success and also highlights once again its divisiveness (Gilbert Youth Research, 1972). The majority of respondents were male (57%), under thirty (70%) and, by the standards of the time, quite highly educated (73% had spent some time at college). Almost all of them appeared to be regular cinemagoers, attending at least once a month, with more than two-thirds saying they had seen at least two films during the previous month.

When asked '[h]ow well you enjoyed the movie', almost half of the respondents under twenty-one chose 'very good'; by contrast only 29% of those over thirty-five selected this answer. Conversely, whereas more than 20% of those over thirty-five found the film 'poor' or 'very poor', only 3% of those under twenty-one did so. A similar, yet less dramatic division can be found in terms of gender. While 42% of males selected 'very good', only 34% of females did, and whereas 12% of women found the film 'poor' or 'very poor', only 6% of men judged the film this way. When asked about their '[r]easons for seeing *Clockwork Orange*', 37% stated that they had '[r]ead good reviews about it' (an option selected especially by those over thirty), while 33% said that '[f]riends/relatives suggested I see it' (an option particularly popular among younger respondents). It would appear that the majority of respondents acted on specific recommendations, either from the press or from people they knew. (With regards to the newspaper boycott, it is also worth mentioning that the majority of respondents had first become aware of *A Clockwork Orange* through newspaper ads.) Importantly, young females were more inclined than any other group to state that they went to see the film because they had been '[j]ust curious', or because 'someone else had wanted to see it', implying that they simply went along with that other person. By contrast, young males were more likely than any other group to declare that they were '[a]ttracted by this kind of movie', by which they mostly expressed a preference for the films of Stanley Kubrick, although some of them also declared that they were attracted by violence.

This survey strongly suggests that, having first seen print ads, potential cinemagoers were immediately divided along the lines of age and gender with regards to their interest in this obviously transgressive film by Stanley Kubrick. Educated young males who habitually went to the cinema were more likely than other groups to act on their interest, and once they had seen the film, it was more probable that they would like it and recommend it to others.[47] In addition to such personal recommendations, good reviews in the press played an important part in motivating people to see the film. The very fact that the film initially received mostly celebratory reviews provoked a strong response from certain film writers and other cultural commentators. It was not only the film's focus on an extremely cruel, yet strangely appealing protagonist, its exhilarating depiction of sex and violence, and its apparent message about both the depravity of man and the importance of free will, which riled its detractors, but also the film's critical and commercial success. For these writers, the huge success of *A Clockwork Orange* had troubling implications for where the American film industry, and indeed American society, were heading. In addition, some writers feared the direct impact *A Clockwork Orange* might have on the more impressionable segments of its audience, especially those who might be inspired to replicate the screen violence in real life. Indeed, an audience survey revealed that the most important segment of the film's audience was male youth. However, unlike Alex and his gang, and also unlike the uneducated ('immature') viewers that even such a strong supporter of the film as Vincent Canby was worried about, the large majority were current or former college students.

The UK Controversy

While the American press only hinted at the possibility that young males in the audience might be moved to violence and crime by *A Clockwork Orange*, this became the dominant theme of the British controversy. Quite surprisingly, the most intense debate about copycat crimes in the UK took place more than a year after the film's London premiere. With few earlier examples, it was only in the spring and summer of 1973 that claims about the film's responsibility for a range of crimes – including attacks on people in the street, gang fights and murder as well as home invasions and rape – gained a lot of exposure in the British press. Before examining the development of the British debate in more detail, it is worth pointing out that the amount of coverage the film received in newspapers and magazines, and also on radio and television, is astounding (it takes up six large-format bound volumes in the Stanley Kubrick Archive), and the diversity of contexts in which the film's title was evoked is also impressive. As time went by, any aspect of British society (by no means only the state of cinema, censorship, youth culture and crime but also, for example, the treatment of prisoners, modern architecture and city planning) could be discussed with reference to *A Clockwork Orange*. I would be surprised to find any other film in recent decades which managed to become as central to public discourse as *A Clockwork Orange* did in the UK in 1972 and 1973. Instead of trying to map out this all-too-extensive discussion in all its breadth and depth, I want to focus quite narrowly on the particular escalation of critical debate which led from the pre-release publicity for this shocking new film by one of Hollywood's great directors to the proliferation of articles about copycat crimes. I think that this escalation is perhaps best understood in terms of a number of distinct, yet closely related themes, which were introduced early on during the film's reception, were then developed with varying degrees of emphasis during subsequent months, and were eventually brought together in claims about a wave of copycat crimes in 1973. I want to go through these themes in the following order: media effects; film as mirror of society; impressionable and wayward youth; youth subcultures; and rising crime rates.

As we saw in Part 3, in the late 1960s, the dramatic liberalisation of film-industry self-regulation and official censorship of films in the US and Britain led to the production of a large number of films featuring previously unseen levels of sexual explicitness and graphically depicted violence. In the UK, the release of such films gave rise to dire warnings about their likely impact on British society. For example, on 6 January 1972, the *Baptist Times*, with particular reference to the most controversial movie of 1971 in the UK – Sam Peckinpah's *Straw Dogs* (cp. Simkin, 2011) – asked the head of the BBFC, Stephen Murphy: 'Has he never heard of imitative behaviour or considered that some people after seeing such films, may well say: "After this, anything goes" – in real life as well as on the screen?' (*Baptist Times*, 1972). The very next day, mentioning both *Straw Dogs* and the forthcoming British release of *A Clockwork Orange* and building on the intense contemporary debate about pornography, the *Sun* wrote: 'films like these, it seems to us, are far more likely to inflame people to violence than conventional pornography is to inflame them to sex' (*Sun*, 1972).[48] On 11 January, another *Sun* article made fun of much academic research on media effects for going against common sense insights about the influence of films: 'Psychologists disagree. Films, they say, cannot influence people and have effect on the moral fibre. Oh, yeah! They can tell that to Dr. Goebbels's old propaganda machine' (Cashin, 1972).

That concerns about the negative impact *A Clockwork Orange* might have on its audiences gained prominence in the UK had a lot to do with the perception that the film held up a mirror to British society. As soon as it had been released in the UK, both the film's supporters and its detractors commented on the fact that its futuristic setting mirrored the social realities of contemporary Britain. (Because American reviewers shared this perception, it was easy for them to play down the film-as-mirror-of-society theme; after all, it was not American society that was being mirrored here.) The film's most vocal supporter in the UK, Alexander Walker, wrote: 'The urban landscape of *Clockwork Orange* is recognisably our own' (Walker, 1972b). In a highly critical article in the Reading *Evening Post*, self-declared liberal Albert Watson acknowledged that the film was quite accurate in showing 'the sort of violence which could become commonplace and everyday if society goes on allowing itself to be brutalised', yet, in his view, *A Clockwork Orange* itself contributed to this brutalisation (Watson, 1972). An article in the Newcastle upon Tyne *Journal* tried to give a balanced account of the various positions in the emerging controversy, once again assuming that, for better or for worse,

A Clockwork Orange was deeply engaged with currents in British culture. It concluded with a question: 'Mirror or moral object lesson? Or gratuitous gloating? Everyone must decide for himself' (Barroch, 1972).

If *A Clockwork Orange* mirrored troubling social realities and if the media had long been assumed to have a negative effect on their audiences, especially youth, then it followed that young viewers were most likely to be influenced by the juvenile delinquency portrayed in *A Clockwork Orange*. Soon after the film's release, an article entitled 'Cinema Violence Renews Yobs' Faith in Bovver Power' predicted that the anti-violence message of *A Clockwork Orange* was 'almost certain to be misunderstood by your Saturday night yob, who will only see that it's fun to rape a woman' (Southworth, 1972). And the article from the Newcastle upon Tyne *Journal* quoted earlier noted: 'it is believed that film violence fans community violence, particularly among the young and impressionable' (Barroch, 1972). Similarly, a Labour MP writing in the London *Evening News* at the end of January predicted that screenings of *A Clockwork Orange* 'will lead to a clockwork cult which will magnify teenage violence' (Edelman, 1972). In this way, the press articulated specific worries about the influence the film might have on young people who, it was assumed, were already engaged, or easily tempted to engage, in antisocial and otherwise questionable behaviour, and who were also regular cinemagoers likely to see the movie.

Worries about impressionable youth in the audience of *A Clockwork Orange* were intensified by reports about a small but growing minority of young people who started copying the film's fashions. A review published in the *Record Mirror* in January 1972 linked the uniform worn by Alex and his droogs to possible shifts in existing youth subcultures: 'I can see whole legions of droogs emerging from the embers of the skinhead movement wearing bowlers, white suits, external jock straps and boots and carrying thick canes' (*Record Mirror*, 1972). Skinheads had been the most recent in a series of subcultural formations among British working-class male youth, which had received a lot of attention since the 1950s. In fact, Teddy Boys in the 1950s, and Mods and Rockers in the 1960s had been the focus of full-fledged moral panics, with excessive claims about their violent behaviour from journalists, judges and politicians, and public calls for various forms of state intervention such as more intense policing, tougher sentencing and new laws (cp. Rock and Cohen, 1970, and Cohen, 1972/2002). Stanley Cohen has shown that subcultural formations arise from the interplay between the fashion, music and behavioural choices of young people and the construction of particular youth-group identities in the media. The more the media draw attention to transgressive youthful looks and behaviour, the more attractive these can become for young people; as a consequence, the actually rather ill-defined and always fluid styles adopted by young people can crystallise into a uniform, and occasional incidents of violence can escalate into riotous behaviour (Rock and Cohen, 1970, and Cohen, 1972/2002).

As a result of such feedback processes, by 1969 working-class teenagers labelled as 'skinheads' had adopted a hypermasculine style:

> large working boots, often with steel toe-caps, denim jeans supported by braces, worn with a gap between the top of the boots and the bottom of the jeans, a coloured or patterned, shaped shirt with a button-down collar. Over this was worn a sleeveless pullover and for colder weather a 'Crombie' overcoat. The outfit was topped with very close cropped hair. (Clarke, 1973, quoted in Kerr, 1994, p. 54)

Skinheads were most notorious for their fighting on football grounds and their racial violence (pp. 54, 81–2; Ingham *et al.*, 1978, Chs 1–2). Looking back on the early 1970s, in 1976 sociologists noted a surprising shift in working-class youth styles, away from the skinhead look to the more effeminate, androgynous look that came to be known as 'glam rock': long hair, flared trousers, colourful shirts and make-up (Taylor and Wall, 1976). In retrospect, the 'droogs' in *A Clockwork Orange* look exactly like a halfway point in this transition, with clothes and boots looking back to the skinheads, and longer hair and make-up looking forward to glam rock (cp. Buovolo, 2004). The film review in the *Record Mirror* quoted earlier seemed to capture this transition as it was happening. And as early as February 1972, the MP James Hill predicted that *Clockwork Orange* fashion would lead to copycat violence: 'by natural progression the violence associated with this costume will be tried out on the innocent public' (Hill, 1972).

However, the youth-subcultures theme did not gain much attention in the writing about *A Clockwork Orange* until the beginning of 1973 when various commentators were looking back on key developments of the previous year, and identified the rise of what would later be called glam rock as one of these developments. Thus, an article in the *Evening News* from 17 January 1973, entitled 'Why Bovver Boys Like the Glitter', observed that young working-class males, including violent ones, were now wearing eye shadow and glitter (Stoddart, 1973). With reference to Slade, Roy Wood, Marc Bolan and David Bowie, the article noted:

> The current move began with rock stars determined to be outrageous. … As far as the heavies were concerned, the final seal of approval was given to make-up by no less a man than Stanley Kubrick, whose ultraviolent hero Alex wears false eyelashes as he bludgeons people to death in *A Clockwork Orange.*

Across 1973, there were numerous reports about the violent and non-violent activities of groups of youngsters wearing droog outfits and often labelled 'Clockwork gangs'; these emerged wherever the film was shown outside London (cp. *Falkirk Herald*, 1973).

For some commentators, it appeared that urban youth culture and juvenile delinquency were spreading out from London to the rest of the country, as seemed to be the case with regards to rising crime rates in general. Across the 1960s and into the 1970s, there was growing concern in the UK about a dramatic increase in crime and the fact that recently enacted 'permissive' laws might make the work of the police and the courts more difficult so that criminals might go unpunished, and the deterrent function of punishment might be much reduced.[49] Some commentators highlighted the corrosive role played, in their view, by popular entertainment in this process. Thus, the *Daily Express* wrote on 18 January 1972: 'the spectacular increase in violent crime, from the late fifties to the present day, has been largely brought about by the crumbling of standards', which in turn had partly been caused by 'pornographers' and 'purveyors of violence' in the media whose works were a form of 'moral pollution' (MacMillan, 1972). When *A Clockwork Orange* went on national release in January 1973, there was anxiety that such moral pollution and associated crimes would spread. For example, when the film was about to be shown in Hereford in February 1973, a resident expressed her concern in the local paper: 'They know that mugging in the East End of London has increased and the number of beatings has trebled after the showing of this film' (Roleston, 1973).

All of these themes – the negative effects of media, *A Clockwork Orange* as a mirror of contemporary Britain, the susceptibility and transgressiveness of youth, the prominence of skinheads, glam rock and 'Clockwork gangs' in British culture, rising crime rates all around the country – fed into concerns about the film's responsibility for copycat crimes. After scattered earlier references in the press to crimes allegedly related to *A Clockwork Orange*, an intensive and sustained public debate about copycat crimes got started with a frontpage article published on 5 April 1973 in the London *Evening News* under the headline 'Mugging Murder in Church Porch' (Godfrey, 1973). The article reported that sixty-year-old David McManus

> died today after being viciously battered … . Police believe the killing may have been inspired by the film *Clockwork Orange*. … In the film, which was shown in Bletchley two weeks ago, an old tramp is savagely beaten by four young thugs.

It seems that the police had no hard evidence, or indeed *any* evidence, to connect the attack on McManus to the film. Yet what the *Evening News* called '[t]he *Clockwork Orange* theory' – that is the assumption that the violence in the film caused violence among young viewers – had by then become such a familiar explanatory framework that it could be applied to any criminal incident. During the next few months, it became increasingly convenient for journalists and the police, the criminals themselves, their parents and attorneys, judges and campaigners to apply the '*Clockwork Orange* theory' to every brutal act that would otherwise seem to be unmotivated. If no obvious explanation for a brutal crime committed by young people existed, then one might as well try out the idea that it had been 'caused', one way or another, by *A Clockwork Orange*.

Conclusion

I want to conclude this part by putting the marketing and reception of *A Clockwork Orange* in a broader context, referring back to the developments in British and American culture and society discussed in Part 3. In many ways, both the film's success and the controversy it caused arose from processes of dramatic change. Most generally, we can note that the 1960s and 1970s have been identified as decades characterised by the rapid liberalisation of attitudes and values, as measured in opinion polls, particularly among young people.[50] These changes in public opinion underpinned the equally rapid liberalisation of the film industry's self-regulation. The newly liberated film industry was thus enabled, and new generations of filmmakers rising to prominence at this time were particularly keen, to produce high-profile films criticising traditional values and major institutions as well as breaking taboos; many of these films became hugely successful at the box office from 1967 onwards.[51] However, it also has to be noted that such films alienated large segments of the population so that by the early 1970s, cinema attendance levels reached their historical low point in the US (Krämer, 2005, pp. 58–62), while in the UK annual ticket sales were almost halved between 1966 and 1972.[52] In particular, graphic depictions of sex and violence escalated in the hit movies of the late 1960s and early 1970s (Krämer, 2005, pp. 47–58) and across American and British cinema in general.[53] The commercial success of *A Clockwork*

Orange can at least partly be explained by this escalation (cp. Krämer, 2010a, and forthcoming a), whereas its success with reviewers was dependent on shifts in Anglo-American film criticism, notably critics' increasing emphasis on cinema as an art form, on directors as artists and on the positive value of filmic transgressions.[54]

While such developments were favourable for the success of *A Clockwork Orange*, both in the US and the UK, there also was a considerable backlash – partly inspired by rising crime rates and widespread concerns about the breakdown of law and order[55] – against liberalising trends in society in general and in cinema in particular. In both countries, the late 1960s and early 1970s were a period of particularly heated public debates about deviant youth and about the impact of violent as well as pornographic media representations on their audiences; these debates gave rise to, and were in turn fed by, large-scale investigations and research efforts, organised by governments, individual politicians, academics and broadcasters.[56] Thus, the same factors that helped the film to achieve great commercial and critical success also contributed to the attacks on it. Indeed, many of the film's detractors seemed to be particularly incensed by the fact that *A Clockwork Orange* was so successful, taking this as a measure of the depth of general cinematic and cultural decline. They also appeared to have been influenced by the very bleakness of the future that the film portrays, and rather than understanding the film as a warning, they were worried that it would help bring this future about. Its attractive portrayal of a juvenile delinquent might inspire young viewers to emulate him (the main focus of the controversy in the UK), while its apparently negative view of human nature in conjunction with its evocation of social chaos might contribute to calls for more authoritarian government, more restrictive legislation and more repressive law-enforcement (a major focus of the US controversy).

 **PART 5**

THE LEGACY OF
A CLOCKWORK ORANGE

Introduction

Under the headline '"Homophobic" Killing: Teenage Girls Attacked Man Like a Scene from *Clockwork Orange*, Jury Told', the *Daily Telegraph* reported in April 2010 on the trial of two young women and a young man (aged eighteen and nineteen), who were alleged to have 'taunted', 'punched', 'kicked and stamped on' a sixty-two-year-old 'homosexual man' who had been taking a walk 'with his friend' in Trafalgar Square (*Daily Telegraph*, 2010). While much of the worst violence appeared to have come from the young man, the actions of the two young women were highlighted throughout the article, especially the fact that they had been drinking heavily and attacked their victim while he was lying on the ground. He died from a brain injury eighteen days later. The prosecutor's reference to *A Clockwork Orange* was perhaps motivated by similarities between the crime and particular film scenes, especially the droogs' mocking, hitting and kicking of a tramp in a public space, but also perhaps the two home invasions, both of which result, more or less directly, in the death of the main victims. However, the article made no effort to outline these similarities; indeed, it gave no information whatsoever about this almost forty-year-old movie. It simply assumed that readers would recognise the film's title and know that the film featured particularly vicious criminal behaviour by young people. This in turn would seem to indicate that *A Clockwork Orange* has become a permanent fixture in British culture. One could say that it is as much a presence in the Britain of the second decade of the twenty-first century as it had been in the United States of 1972, when, as we saw at the very beginning of this book, the *New York Times* referenced the film to illustrate the viciousness of a particular real-life crime. In today's Britain, the film continues to be used regularly for illustrative purposes, while the claim, made at the height of the British controversy surrounding the film in 1973, that it causes young people to commit crimes is much less likely to be repeated.

In this final part of the book, I examine the film's legacy in three ways. First, I survey the vast literature about *A Clockwork Orange* which film critics and film scholars, mainly from the UK and the US, have produced since the 1970s. This literature helped to cement the film's place in contemporary culture. Second, I discuss the peculiar exhibition history of *A Clockwork Orange* in the UK. The film was not legally available in this country from 1974 to 2000, which arguably increased its reputation and cultural impact. Finally, I look at some of the research that has been done on how actual audiences have responded to, and made use of, *A Clockwork Orange* in contemporary Britain.

Film Criticism and Film Studies

The amount of academic writing about *A Clockwork Orange* is impressive, even a bit overwhelming for anyone – such as myself – who sets out to produce a new piece of writing about the film which should, of course, be grounded at least in a basic, and ideally in a very intimate, familiarity with all that has already been said about it by other scholars. Even if we restrict ourselves only to English-language publications (as I mostly did, with the exception of a few publications in German), there is a lot of ground to cover. I have already referenced some of the academic writing in the preceding parts of this book, and here I merely want to provide a brief historical survey of this literature, starting with specialist high-brow film journals, which are positioned halfway between the mainstream press and academic publications. The interest of such journals in *A Clockwork Orange* was intense from the very beginning, which had, I think, a lot to do with the fact that, by 1971, Stanley Kubrick had already been recognised as one of the most important filmmakers in Hollywood, indeed in the world, and his latest offering was seen to deserve a lot of attention, both through critical analyses and through conversations with Kubrick. Hence we find interviews in the American journal *Take One*

(Hofsess, 1971/2001) and the British journal *Sight and Sound* (Strick and Houston, 1972/2001). The latter also published a series of extensive critical essays on *A Clockwork Orange*, both during the film's long run in British cinemas (Strick, 1971/1972, and Daniels, 1972/1973) and afterwards (e.g. Moskowitz, 1976/1977). While some of these essays defended the film against attacks, Charles Barr's comparative analysis of the initial reception of *Straw Dogs* and *A Clockwork Orange* by London reviewers contrasted the critical condemnation of the former with the critical celebration of the latter, and challenged the grounds on which these judgments about the films were made (Barr, 1972). Given the usual time lag for academic publications, it is astonishing that this study appeared in what was at the time the leading Film Studies journal in Britain, perhaps in the world, within only a few months of the film's release. Barr's piece was a major inspiration for the most extensive scholarly analysis of *A Clockwork Orange* published in the 1970s, Thomas Elsaesser's thirty-page-long chapter for Christopher Bigsby's *Approaches to Popular Culture*, one of the foundational British anthologies on the study of popular culture (Elsaesser, 1976).[57] The central theme of most of these essays – and also of critical analyses appearing in *The Velvet Light Trap* at that time (Evans, 1974, and Moskowitz, 1976) – was, not surprisingly, the film's representation of violence. Another important focus of early discussions, often overlapping with the interest in violence, was the film's relationship to Burgess's novel (e.g., Gilbert, 1974; Gumenik, 1972; Isaac, 1973). In this context, we can also find an early feminist critique of the film's representation of women (Walker, 1972).

The publications I have mentioned so far were motivated by, and focused on, the film and/or the controversy surrounding it. After the 1970s, such publications became much rarer, and the vast majority of writing about *A Clockwork Orange* could now be found in books about Stanley Kubrick, most of which covered all of his work and therefore automatically included material on *A Clockwork Orange*. While free-standing essays also often related the film to Kubrick's other work, such connections became more important when *A Clockwork Orange* was discussed in a book about the director. There were quite a few such books on Kubrick in the 1970s and early 1980s.[58] Whether written by academics or by journalists, they tended to address a general readership rather than a scholarly audience; some of them were produced in consultation with the filmmaker, and several would appear in new editions in subsequent decades. After a dearth of books about Kubrick from the mid-1980s to the early 1990s, the years 1994–9 saw the appearance of several new volumes,[59] including the first in-depth biographies (LoBrutto, 1998; Baxter, 1998). Apart from the biographies, these books were written by, and addressed primarily to, academics; all of them included either substantial chapters about, or at least numerous scattered references to, *A Clockwork Orange*. After Kubrick's death in 1999, the publishing floodgates really opened. Updated editions of older books appeared,[60] as well as a wealth of new books, including academic monographs[61] and edited collections,[62] but also a range of books addressed to a general readership.[63] In addition to the extensive discussions of *A Clockwork Orange* in such books, the film has once again become the focus of various publications which are solely dedicated to its examination; these include an edited collection as well as several journal essays and book chapters.[64] As in the first series of essays in the 1970s, violence is a major theme in recent critical writing about *A Clockwork Orange*, and the film's relationship with the novel also continues to be an important topic. In addition, more attention than before has been paid to questions of form and style, to the complex ways in which *A Clockwork Orange* engages its audience, and to the broader philosophical and political implications of its story.

Most of the literature discussed in the previous paragraph was written by North American scholars. Where that literature situated Kubrick's work in general, and *A Clockwork Orange* in particular, in the context of cinematic traditions, the main reference points were Hollywood cinema and international art cinema. However, in the last few years, there has also been an increasing emphasis, mainly on the part of British scholars, on the place of *A Clockwork Orange* in British film history.[65] In addition to examining the film's generic affiliations as well as non-filmic British cultural influences on its production, this scholarship is particularly interested in the controversy surrounding *A Clockwork Orange* in the UK and the 'cult' audience it has attracted there. As we saw, as early as 1972, Charles Barr had examined the film's critical reception in London.[66] Soon thereafter, *A Clockwork Orange* featured prominently in books about film-industry self-regulation and official censorship in the UK.[67] Such work has been continued in recent years,[68] and is now being complemented by research into responses to the film by viewers in contemporary Britain.[69] Importantly, these publications have helped to ensure that *A Clockwork Orange* remains central to discussions of media effects and film censorship in the UK, and they both reflect, and contribute to, its elevated status among fans of 'cult' movies in this country. Thus, when Karl French, with a general readership in mind, put together a collection of essays on the ever-topical issue of 'screen violence' in 1996, two of his contributors (Mary Whitehouse and Tony Parsons) wrote extensively about *A Clockwork Orange* (the former attacking it, the latter celebrating it). And when, in 2001, Ali Catterall and Simon Wells published their book on British cult movies since the 1960s, which is addressed precisely to the fans of such films, they introduced their long chapter on Kubrick's movie as follows: 'In this small quirky canon of British cult movies, *A Clockwork Orange* is regarded, almost by default, as among the "cultiest"' (p. 102).

At the same time, the continuing attention paid by British film scholars and film journalists to Kubrick's movie has prepared the ground for it becoming a noticeable presence in the increasingly extensive and indeed popular literature about Britain in the 1970s. Such books tend to dedicate several pages to *A Clockwork Orange* and the controversy surrounding it (e.g. Sounes, 2007, pp. 124–8; Turner, 2008, pp. 74–5; and Sandbrook, 2010, pp. 447–9). When such historians reach out for an even wider audience with television documentaries, *A Clockwork Orange* lends itself to being featured prominently. Thus, already the pre-credit sequence of the third episode of *Andrew Marr's History of Modern Britain* (BBC, 2007) includes clips from *A Clockwork Orange* and three minutes of this sixty-minute programme are taken up by a discussion of the film and the reactions it provoked. In this way, *A Clockwork Orange* can easily be made to stand in not only for early 1970s British cinema,[70] but also for the country as a whole, the film's grim vision of the future perfectly in line with today's grim perspective on Britain in the 1970s, and the intensity of conflict within its story and in the public debate about the film an apparently perfect expression of social, cultural and political divisions during that decade.

As I have shown in this book, *A Clockwork Orange* is indeed deeply rooted in British culture – but it is the culture of the 1950s as much as that of the 1970s. At the same time, it is important to consider that the film arose at a specific moment in Hollywood history and in Stanley Kubrick's career. Indeed, I have tried to show that there are a wide range of historical contexts in which we can place this film and also the controversy surrounding it, in the same way as there are many levels at which it operates as a cultural artefact, offering diverse meanings and pleasures. Neither this book nor the enormous amount of previous writing about *A Clockwork Orange* has in any way exhausted what it has to offer. There is so much more to be learnt about the film's themes, form and style, its production history as well as its marketing and reception in the UK, the US and the rest of the world. Much of this can be investigated with the help of the filmmaker's very extensive and diverse personal collection of documents and artefacts, which is now accessible at the Stanley Kubrick Archive at the University of the Arts London. It is worth pointing out that, in my experience, the more one watches the film and the more one reads about it (in the scholarly literature, popular accounts or archival records), the more there seems to be to say about it. Thus, we can conclude that an important legacy of *A Clockwork Orange* is the continuing and open-ended debate, between scholars, journalists, fans and regular viewers, about the film's origins, meanings, pleasures and impact. Much like the initial controversy about the film, this debate is more intense in the UK than in the US, which, among other things, has a lot to do with its peculiar exhibition history in this country.

The Film's Withdrawal and Re-release in the UK

Under the headline '*Clockwork Orange* London Perennial, Now in Third Year', an article in the American trade press reported in January 1974 that the film was still playing in the capital, having generated 'phenomenal' box-office revenues during its extraordinarily long run (*Daily Variety*, 1974). However, as happens to all films eventually, at some point over the next few months it had played out in the UK, finally being replaced everywhere with newer releases. Yet its run in the British press went on; *A Clockwork Orange* continued to be referenced regularly in articles about court cases involving young criminals, about the BBFC and censorship, about the state of cinema and, indeed, about the state of the nation.[71] As could be expected for a major hit movie, within a few years Warner Bros. started planning a major international re-release for the film. At that point, in January 1976, Stanley Kubrick wrote to the distributor asking them to 're-adjust the plan', and within a week Warner Bros. had dropped the UK from the re-release schedule (Kubrick, 1976; Eriksson, 1976). The correspondence does not reveal why Kubrick asked for this change, nor did Kubrick or Warner Bros. officially explain why the film was, from then on, withheld not only from cinemas in the UK, but also from video and television, so that it could not be seen legally in this country for decades.[72] Even without an official explanation, it was widely understood that, in the wake of the controversy surrounding the film in the UK, in particular the accusations that it – and thus its maker – was responsible for a series of copycat crimes, Kubrick and his family had received threats, and that Kubrick had therefore 'banned' the film in this country. Warner Bros. made sure that there were no exceptions. In March 1993, *The Times* (London) reported – under the somewhat misleading headline 'Cinema Breached Kubrick Copyright' – that during the previous year the Scala cinema in London had got hold of a print of *A Clockwork Orange* and screened it 'without the permission of Warner Bros.', thus 'breaching copyright' – which was held by the company, not by Kubrick (Londale, 1993; cp. Catterall and Wells, 2001, pp. 117–18). The cinema had been sued by the Federation Against Copyright

Theft (FACT), and on 23 March 1993, the court ruled in FACT's favour. A representative of the organisation stated: 'The fact that it was *A Clockwork Orange* had nothing to do with it. We would have taken the action even had it been any other film.' The same year Warner Bros. challenged the inclusion of extensive clips from *A Clockwork Orange* in a British television documentary on censorship (entitled *Forbidden Fruit*), once again on the grounds of breach of copyright, yet this time the court ruled against the distributor and the programme was broadcast with those clips on Channel 4 in October 1993, and later uses of *A Clockwork Orange* clips in documentaries went unchallenged (Parsons, 1996, p. 185; Hughes, 2000, p. 171). These legal actions, which appeared to be rather heavy-handed, added to the mystique of the film, enhancing its status as a 'forbidden fruit', and there is anecdotal evidence suggesting that for many a (usually male) British youngster seeing a foreign video of the film, often a second- or third-generation bootleg copy, became an important rite of passage (Parsons, 1996, p. 182; Catterall and Wells, 2001, p. 117).

When the distributor finally got ready for the film's theatrical re-release in the UK after Kubrick's death in March 1999, Warner Bros. executive Julian Senior belatedly gave an official explanation for the film's long absence from British screens: 'Stanley did receive threats from strange people. And it was because of this that we withdrew the film, but only in Britain. He also stopped the video being released [in the UK] (Lister, 1999). 'It was not a ban but a decision by Stanley Kubrick, the police and Warner Brothers. The police were saying to us: "We think you should do something about this. It is getting dangerous"' (Travis, 1999). Kubrick's brother-in-law Jan Harlan, who had worked on all of his films since *A Clockwork Orange*, said: 'He never had any legal right to ban it, but Warner Brothers wanted to oblige him' (McCann, 1999). It is worth pointing out how unusual it is that Warner Bros. relinquished one of the world's largest film markets to please a filmmaker – but, then again, it is equally unusual that, from *A Clockwork Orange* onwards, for almost thirty years Kubrick only made films for Warner Bros. *A Clockwork Orange* was given a surprisingly wide release in March

2000, being shown on 328 screens in the UK, and earning £619,000 at the box office during its first weekend, which the British trade paper *Screen International* judged to be 'a respectable showing for what is essentially an art-house movie' (O'Sullivan, 2000). It is unclear whether the designation 'art-house movie' merely referred to the fact that this was an old movie rather than a current release, or whether it indicated that the critical parameters delineating contemporary cinema had shifted so much that one of the biggest box-office hits in early 1970s Britain could no longer fit into the 'mainstream' category as it was understood in the early 2000s. Be that as it may, in July 2001, *A Clockwork Orange* was finally shown in full on British television, albeit only to a limited audience as a pay-per-view offering on Sky Box Office (*New York Post*, 2001). Since then the film has been shown numerous times on free TV and become available on video and DVD in the UK. In this way, *A Clockwork Orange* has been able to reach an astonishingly broad audience in contemporary Britain.

The Film's Audiences

At the beginning of the new millennium, the British Board of Film Classification commissioned a study of the 'attitudes and reactions of video renters to sexual violence in film' (Cumberbatch, 2002). A cross-section of customers of video-rental outlets in the Midlands were surveyed through a questionnaire, and a smaller sample of people was then invited to screenings of, and interviewed about, a range of older and recent films featuring sexual violence, among them *A Clockwork Orange* (p. 1). The people filling in the questionnaire and being interviewed included men and women, the young (but not younger than sixteen) and the old, the educated and the uneducated (pp. 4, 9). While they were not strictly speaking representative of the British population (over fifteen) as a whole, their responses can be understood as an indication of general trends. Perhaps the most important result for our purposes is that in 2002, only two years after the British re-release of

A Clockwork Orange, an astonishing 47% of male respondents said that they had seen the film (the figure for female respondents was 37%), while another 25% (24% for females) said that, although they had not seen it, they knew a lot about it (p. 13). Only 8% of male respondents (18% of females) said they knew nothing about *A Clockwork Orange* (p. 13). The respondents' level of familiarity with *A Clockwork Orange* was much higher than it was for all the other films the survey asked about, with the exception of *Reservoir Dogs* (1991) and *Saving Private Ryan* (1998). In addition, the film had 'the lowest number of negative appraisals (19%)' of all films shown to the smaller sample (the other films were *Straw Dogs*, 1971; *The Last House on the Left*, 1972; *I Spit on Your Grave*, 1978; *Death Wish II*, 1982; and *Baise-Moi*, 2000) and 'the highest number of positive comments (68%)' (p. 29). This despite the fact that 44% of respondents agreed (most of them 'strongly') with the statement that '[f]orcible sex with a woman is presented as exciting and attractive' in the film (p. 29). At the same time, the majority (51%) disagreed with the statement that '[t]he main character Alex … is presented as an attractive role model' (p. 30). Together with some of the interview statements of respondents, this would seem to suggest that they felt that the film's depiction of sexual violence was enjoyable (enjoyable for Alex and through him for the audience), but this was done, in their view, in a thought-provoking rather than a harmful fashion, the film encouraging viewers to be critical of Alex's behaviour. While a substantial portion of respondents (between 25% and 50%) were concerned about the negative impact that sexually violent videos or, more generally, media violence might have on audience attitudes and behaviour, only very few thought that films such as *A Clockwork Orange* 'might encourage copycat behaviour' (p. 59).

When, in the academic year 2002–3, Martin Barker and Ernest Mathijs examined the responses of British first-year students to *A Clockwork Orange* (through questionnaires and discussions), they found them to be overwhelmingly positive:

> The majority of respondents (55%) positioned themselves as having enjoyed and admired *A Clockwork Orange*, while less than one out of

five (16.2%) gave negative responses on either dimension [enjoyment, admiration]. Only eight respondents placed themselves on the negative pole of both axes. ... [T]hese results would seem to confirm the status of *A Clockwork Orange* as a 'masterpiece of cinema': a film that manages to deliver pleasure to its audiences, while also earning respect for how that pleasure ... is realized. (Barker and Mathijs, 2005, p. 52)

The researchers noted that 'supporting comments offered for the positive response ... emphasised the aesthetic appeal of the film', or ' the theme(s) of the film' (to do mostly with questions of morality, violent behaviour and the role of the state) – but rarely both (pp. 53–4). Whatever the focus of students' comments was, and however they judged the film, most of them agreed that *A Clockwork Orange* was 'disturbing' (p. 54). For a few, this meant that they were unsettled, even sickened by the film without being able to give this experience any meaning that could justify it; for most respondents, however, being disturbed was closely tied to an ultimately enjoyable visceral response and/or to an intellectual engagement with the film's themes: 'the most positive responses combine some strong, viscerally excited reactions with equally powerful cognitive responses' (p. 54). Finally, while older respondents might recall that, when the film was first released, some of their schoolfriends dressed up as droogs and that the film had been 'banned' for a long time, they did not seem to find it worth mentioning that *A Clockwork Orange* had been held responsible for copycat crimes (pp. 57–8).

In his examination of fan discourse about *A Clockwork Orange* on the internet, Justin Smith notes that contributors (who, judging by the American spelling used in their postings, were mostly from the US) were heavily invested in the film's style, revelling in the immediacy of its impact every time they saw the film, but also, in some cases, trying to find ways to incorporate aspects of that style into their everyday lives (2010a, p. 157). At the same time, fans tended to emphasise the important role *A Clockwork Orange* had played in their lives from the moment they had first seen it (which would usually appear to have been during their teenage years). Smith writes:

They celebrate the film in a spirit of nostalgia for its iconic presentation of violence, its visceral nihilism, projecting back to an imagined moment when youth rebellion might have had teeth and been given certain credence. But it is emphatically also a resource: a milestone … on their own personal rite of passage. (Smith, 2010b, p. 84)

Conclusion

I want to conclude this book by going back to the time when *A Clockwork Orange* was first presented to audiences. As we saw in Part 4, according to a survey conducted during the film's initial release in the US, *A Clockwork Orange* was mostly seen by young people, the majority of whom enjoyed it, most especially educated males. The Stanley Kubrick Archive contains a wide range of letters written in response to the first encounter with *A Clockwork Orange* by regular cinemagoers (rather than by people professionally involved in film criticism or filmmaking), mostly Americans, during 1971–2 (cp. Krämer, 2011). While the majority of correspondents are young and/or male, other demographic groups are represented as well. Almost all of the letters are very positive, celebrating the film's style, exploring its themes, or both. And some offer passionate, perceptive and thoughtful accounts both of the film and of the letter writer's complex engagement with it. Because I hope that this book will encourage readers to return to *A Clockwork Orange* so as to explore both the film and themselves, I end with a discussion of one of these letters.

In March 1972, a woman from Ohio wrote to Kubrick about her two viewings of *A Clockwork Orange*.[73] She first saw the film at a 'private showing for … a select audience', which she characterises as 'the intelligentsia'. While 'I usually don't like violent movies', in the case of *A Clockwork Orange*, the music helped her enjoy the film, and in any case 'I didn't mind the violence because it seemed so much like fantasy that I couldn't be brought into it.' However, during her second viewing of the film, the scene in which Alex, after

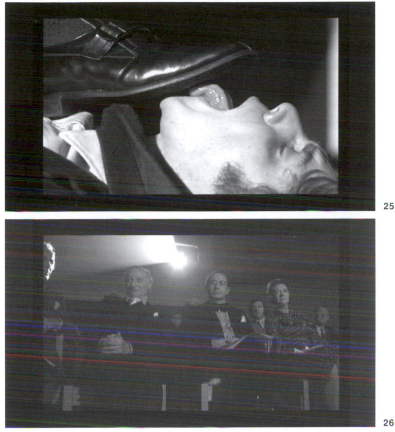

25

26

the completion of the Ludovico treatment, is presented as a reformed
individual (who licks an aggressor's boot rather than fighting back) to an
audience of dignitaries and reporters (figs. 25–6) had unpleasant echoes of the
very situation in which she had first seen the film: 'a select audience gathered
together to cooly [sic] observe violence and sex and graciously applauded ... .
They were divorced from the human interplay on the stage, just as I was from
the violent interactions of the movie.'

The parallels between the film scene and the reality of the viewing situation alerted her to the fact that the film was no 'futuristic' 'fantasy', but had to do with the 'here and now' of her own life, telling her:

> You have been desensitized to humans so terribly that you no longer believe what you see to be real. Other people appear only to be mere objects. Alex did not feel for his victims, but then neither did you.

In other words, this woman was concerned about the fact that it had been all too easy for her to be like Alex and like the audience to whom he is displayed in the film, that is, it was all too easy not to care for the suffering of characters in the film; after all they are not real. Yet, she went further by suspecting that, for whatever reason, it had become commonplace to play down, or doubt, the reality of other people's lives *outside* the cinema, and thus to disregard *real* suffering. As a result of her reflections on viewing *A Clockwork Orange*, she hoped to be able to inoculate herself against the dangerous perception that life is 'like a play and other people are merely actors'. This is, I think, an important issue which reaches well beyond the debates about *A Clockwork Orange* in particular and about film violence in general. Rather than losing ourselves in discussions about films, about their meanings, effects and uses, we need to remind ourselves – and indeed let the films remind us – that ultimately what should concern us is not filmic representation but the reality of suffering in our own world.

 APPENDICES

Appendix A: Key Details

Taken from the film's end credits as reproduced in Kubrick (1972/2000), and Kubrick (2002, pp. 183–4); several minor items have been dropped. The additional information at the bottom is taken from a variety of sources.

Produced and directed by Stanley Kubrick
Screenplay by Stanley Kubrick
Based on the novel by Anthony Burgess

Cast

Starring

Alex	Malcolm McDowell		Mr Alexander	Patrick Magee

And featuring in alphabetical order

Chief Guard	Michael Bates		Deltoid	Aubrey Morris
Dim	Warren Clarke		Prison Chaplain	Godfrey Quigley
Stage Actor	John Clive		Mum	Sheila Raynor
Mrs Alexander	Adrienne Corri		Dr Branom	Madge Ryan
Dr Brodsky	Carl Duering		Conspirator	John Savident
Tramp	Paul Farrell		Minister of the Interior	Anthony Sharp
Lodger	Clive Francis		Dad	Philip Stone
Prison Governor	Michael Gover		Psychiatrist	Pauline Taylor
Catlady	Miriam Karlin		Conspirator	Margaret Tyzack
Georgie	James Marcus			

Executive Producers	Max L. Raab and Si Litvinoff		Associate Producer	Bernard Williams
			Assistant to the Producer	Jan Harlan
Consultant on Hair and Colouring	Leonard of London			

Electronic music composed and realised by Walter Carlos
Symphony No. 9 in D Minor, Opus 125 by Ludwig van Beethoven
Overtures *The Thieving Magpie* and *William Tell* by Gioachino Rossini
Pomp and Circumstance Marches Nos 1 and 4 by Edward Elgar
'Singin' in the Rain' by Arthur Freed and Nacio Herb Brown from the MGM picture
performed by Gene Kelly
Overture to the Sun composed by Terry Tucker
'I Want to Marry a Lighthouse Keeper' composed and performed by Erika Eigen

Production crew

Lighting Cameraman	John Alcott	Wardrobe Supervisor	Ron Beck
Production Designer	John Barry	Costume Designer	Milena Canonero
Editor	Bill Butler	Stunt Arranger	Roy Scammell
Sound Editor	Brian Blamey	Special Paintings and	Herman Makkink,
Sound Recordist	John Jordan	Sculpture	Cornelius Makkink,
Dubbing Mixers	Bill Rowe, Eddie Haben		Liz Moore,
Art Directors	Russell Hagg, Peter Sheilds		Christiane Kubrick

Made at Pinewood Studios, London, at EMI-MGM Studios, Borehamwood, Hertfordshire,
and on location in England by Hawk Films Limited
Distributed by Warner Bros.

Additional information

Running time: 136 minutes
Release dates: 19 December 1971 (US), 13 January 1972 (UK)
Ratings: 'X' in the US (MPAA certificate dated 15 December 1971) and the UK (BBFC
certificate dated 15 December 1971), slightly modified version rated 'R' in the US for
theatrical re-release (MPAA certificate dated 22 August 1972), rated '18' for UK theatrical
re-release in 2000 and for UK video and DVD release in 2001

Appendix B: Notes

1 For example, Leyton, 1986; Baumeister, 1996; Rhodes, 1999; Gilligan, 2000; Kekes, 2005, esp. Chs 5 and 7; Cole, 2008; and Taylor, 2009; on rape in particular see, for example, Allison and Wrightsman, 1993, and Bourke, 2008. Cp. Stratton, 1996.
2 Cp. the massive bibliography in a recent survey of social-science research on media violence in Potter, 1999, pp. 257–85.
3 For example, Barker and Petley, 1997; Bok, 1998; Heins, 2001, esp. Ch. 10; Staiger, 2005, Chs 2 and 7; Trend, 2007; and Butsch, 2008, Ch. 6.
4 For example, Buckingham, 1996; Hill, 1997; Barker and Brooks, 1998; Morrison, 1999; Barker, Arthurs and Harindranath, 2001; Jones, 2002; Barker, 2005 and 2006; and Donovan, 2010.
5 For example, Best, 1989; Goode and Ben-Yehuda, 1994; and Critcher, 2003.
6 For example, Freedman, 1987; Chauncey, 1993; Jenkins, 1992, 1994 and 1998; Best 1990 and 1999.
7 For historical overviews of such debates see Pearson, 1983 and 1984; West, 1988; Boëthius, 1995; and Murdock, 1997. Also see Rock and Cohen, 1970; Barker, 1984a; Gilbert, 1986; Cohen, 1997; and Beaty, 2005, on debates in the 1950s, as well as Barker, 1984b; and Egan, 2007, on the early 1980s.
8 See Rock and Cohen, 1970; Cohen, 1972/2002; Hall *et al.*, 1978; Pearson, 1984; Gilbert, 1986; Boëthius, 1995; Cohen, 1997; Springhall, 1998; and Beaty, 2005. Also see many of the chapters in Gelder and Thornton, 1997.
9 For academic interpretations along these lines, see, for example, Gehrke, 2001; Shaw, 2007; and Winchell, 2008, Ch. 8.
10 In the novel, during the first home invasion, Alex finds a manuscript entitled 'A Clockwork Orange' which Frank Alexander is working on. In it he reads the following passage:

> The attempt to impose upon man, a creature of growth and capable of sweetness, to ooze juicily at the last round the bearded lips of God, to attempt to impose, I say, laws and conditions appropriate to a mechanical creation, against this I raise my sword-pen. (Burgess, 1962/1972, p. 21)

Remembering this, Alex shouts in protest during the presentation that follows the completion of the Ludovico treatment: 'Where do I come into all this? Am I like just some animal or dog? … Am I just to be like a clockwork orange?' (p. 100). When Alex returns to Frank Alexander's house, he reads the writer's by-now published book *A Clockwork Orange*:

> what seemed to come out of it was that all lewdies [people] nowadays were being turned into machines … F. Alexander seemed to think that we all like grow on what he called the world tree in the world-orchard that like Bog or God planted. (p. 124)

Also see Alex's intriguing reference to the phrase 'clockwork orange' when he listens to Bach: 'I began to pony [understand] better what that meant now' (p. 30).

11 In addition to the narrative analysis I am conducting here, it might also be fruitful to examine how the film systematically disappoints generic expectations. One could look at the teen film, in particular the juvenile-delinquency movie (McGee and Robertson, 1982; Considine, 1985, Part IV; and Doherty, 1988, Ch. 5) as well as related film types such as the gang movie and the biker movie (Sobchak, 1982; Rubin, 1994). Furthermore, one could examine *A Clockwork Orange*'s relationship to the prison movie (Querry, 1973; Rafter, 2000, Ch. 5; and Brown, 2009, Ch. 3) and to movies about psychopathic criminals (who are usually portrayed as serial killers; see Douglass, 1981; Rubin, 1992; and Jenkins, 1994, pp. 82–5). As far as Alex's victimisation in large parts of the film and also the revenge of his victims are concerned, it might be fruitful to discuss *A Clockwork Orange* in relation to Thomas Leitch's analysis of the 'victim film' (2002, Ch. 4). These references all relate to American cinema; for generic traditions in British crime films, see, for example, Chibnall and Murphy, 1999. For quantitative content analyses of hit movies featuring crime from the 1940s to the 1980s, see Powers, Rothman and Rothman, 1996, Ch. 5 (for the US); and Reiner, Livingstone and Allen, 2000 (for the UK). In addition to crime-related genres, it is also possible to situate *A Clockwork Orange* within the history of science-fiction cinema, especially its dystopian variant (see, for example, Anderson, 1985; Sobchak, 1987; and Telotte, 2001; as well as, for the UK, Hunter, 1999).

12 Once again, I am using timings for the American DVD version playing at twenty-four frames per second.

13 For analyses of the important role of music in the film, see, for example, Rabinowitz, 2003; and McQuiston, 2008.

14 For a discussion of the film's costume design, see Buovolo, 2004.

15 One assumes that the four droogs are quite young, although perhaps not as young as the schoolboys they are later revealed to be. When the film was shot, the age of the four actors ranged from nineteen to twenty-seven. Malcolm McDowell (Alex) was born on 13 June 1943.

16 Alex's voiceover states at the very beginning of Scene 18: 'This is the real weepy and like tragic part of the story beginning.' It would therefore make sense to start Part 2 with Scene 18, especially since in Scene 17, Alex, although already in police custody, is physically violent to another person for the last time in this film (he grabs the crotch of one of the police officers). Nevertheless, I decided to include Scene 17 in Part 2 because

Alex's official punishment begins here – right after Dim 'punishes' Alex for beating and cutting him in earlier scenes.

17 Biographical information in this section is taken from Biswell, 2005 (which includes a detailed listing of Burgess's publications on pp. 399–411); and Lewis, 2002 (which includes a useful chronology on pp. xv–xxxv). For background information on Lewis, which goes some way towards explaining the very idiosyncratic approach he takes in his Burgess biography, see Lewis, 2009. For a comprehensive listing of publications by and about Burgess up to the late 1970s, see Brewer, 1980. According to Biswell (p. 250), Burgess wrote *A Clockwork Orange* from April to August 1961.

18 Another important approach to the novel, which I am not going to pursue, focuses on its theological dimension, which is central to much of Burgess's writing and therefore also to Burgess criticism. See, for example, Aggeler, 1979, Ch. 5. For a detailed analysis of the book's language, see for example, Sorlin, 2009, pp. 48–53. A glossary of 'nadsat', based on the one included in the 1965 American paperback edition of *A Clockwork Orange*, published by Ballantine, can be found in McDougal, 2003, pp. 141–9.

19 For detailed analyses of the complex connections between these four novels, see, for example, Morris, 1971, pp. 55–75; and DeVitis, 1972, pp. 103–18. Roger Lewis also discusses the influence of a French novel Burgess had just translated into English, *Les Nouveaux Aristocrates* by Michel de Saint-Pierre, first published in 1960, with the English version appearing under the title *The New Aristocrats* in 1962 (Lewis, 2002, pp. 289–93).

20 Cp. Hebdige, 1988, Ch. 3; Osgerby, 1998, Chs 1–5; Sandbrook, 2006, Chs 12–13; Fowler, 2008, Chs 5–6. On the prehistory of the modern teenager, see Savage, 2008. For an account of sexual liberalisation in 50s Britain, see Willetts, 2010.

21 Scott, 1956–7, pp. 20–1; for another study of London crime, including juvenile delinquency in 1960, see Downes, 1966, Chs 6–7.

22 On media reports and public debates about 'Teddy Boys', see Rock and Cohen, 1970. For discussions of their style, see Fyvel, 1963/1997; and Hebdige, 1979, pp. 49–51, 80–4. Also see Downes, 1966, pp. 116–29; Jefferson, 1975/1993, pp. 67–70; Pearson, 1983, Ch. 2; Osgerby, 1998, pp. 119–23, and Fowler, 2008, pp. 109–12, 116–18. The first edition of the book from which the above Fyvel extract on 'Teddy Boy' style is taken was published in 1961, and its title – *The Insecure Offenders: Rebellious Youth in the Welfare State* – seems so appropriate for what Burgess was dealing with in *A Clockwork Orange* that one wonders whether he had read this study.

23 Many such reports are contained in the subject folder, 'Young People: Effects of Films on', in the library of the British Film Institute. Cp. Rock and Cohen, 1970, pp. 310–12. On rock'n'roll movies, see Doherty, 1988, Ch. 4; and Medovoi, 2005, Ch. 3.

24 Once again, see the BFI subject folder 'Young People: Effects of Films on'.

25 See Phelps, 1975; Robertson, 1989, pp. 104–10, 113–16; Aldgate, 1995, Ch. 2; Biltereyst, 2005. Cp. the British campaign against horror comics from the late 1940s to the mid-1950s; Barker, 1984a; and Springhall, 1998, pp. 141–6.

26 On mind-altering drugs in the 1940s and 1950s, see, for example, Greenberg, 2011, Chs 8–9. On the treatment of sex offenders and mental patients, see Bourke, 2007, Ch. 6;

and Greenberg, 2011, Chs 7–9. On brainwashing, see Biderman, 1962; Taylor, 2004; Streatfeild, 2007; and Carruthers, 2009, Ch. 5. On the most famous story about brainwashing in this period – Richard Condon's 1959 novel *The Manchurian Candidate*, which was turned into a movie in 1962 – see Carruthers, 1998, and Jacobson and Gonzalez, 2006. According to Taylor (2004, p. 6), the term brainwashing was widely and metaphorically applied, as a form of criticism, to all kinds of social phenomena by the late 1950s.

27 Page references are to the Penguin edition of 1972, which is a paperback version of the hardback first published by William Heinemann in 1962 (Burgess, 1962/1972).

28 See Gilbert, 1986; and Beaty, 2005. For comparisons between the different formations of, and debates about, delinquent youth cultures in the US and the UK, see Downes, 1966; Campbell, Munce and Galea, 1982; and Stratton, 1985/1997.

29 For more on Mailer, hipster rebels and their place in American literary culture and 50s conceptions of masculinity, see, for example, Ehrenreich, 1983, Ch. 5; Leland, 2004, Ch. 6; and Medovoi, 2005, esp. Chs 1–2, 6.

30 On public debates about psychopathology, in particular sexual psychopaths, in the 1940s and 1950s, see Freedman, 1987; Chauncey, 1993; Jenkins, 1998, Chs 3–5; and Bourke, 2008, Ch. 10. On popular novels and films dealing with psychopathic criminals during this period, see Douglass, 1981; Jenkins, 1994, pp. 82–6; and Cohan, 1997, Ch. 3. For feminist critiques of discourses about psychopaths and sex crime, see Caputi, 1988; and Cameron and Frazer, 1987, esp. Ch. 2.

31 For more on James Dean, *Rebel without a Cause* and juvenile-delinquency movies of the 1950s, see, among many others, Considine, 1985, Ch. 9; Gilbert, 1986, Ch. 11; Doherty, 1988; McCann, 1991, Chs 4 and 5; Cohan, 1997, Ch. 6; Medovoi, 2005, Chs 4–5, 7; and Slocum, 2005.

32 Cp. reprints of the original Production Code and various revisions in, for example, Steinberg, 1980, pp. 390–8; Doherty, 2007, pp. 351–63; and Tropiani, 2009, pp. 271–85, 295–300.

33 See, for example, Leff and Simmons, 1990, Chs 6–10; Lewis, 2000, Ch. 3; Doherty, 2007, Chs 11–14; Sandler, 2007, pp. 25–35; Tropiani, 2009, pp. 51–89.

34 See Leff and Simmons, 1990, Ch. 11; Walsh, 1996, pp. 312–13; Black, 1998, pp. 229–32; Leff, 1998; Tropiani, 2009, pp. 138–42.

35 In contrast to the importance of working-class youth in the UK, US attendance levels were highest among educated middle-class youth (Jowett, 1976, pp. 476–7).

36 On the introduction and implementation of the ratings system, see Farber, 1972; Leff and Simmons, 1990, pp. 269–79; Lewis, 2000, Ch. 4; Vaughn, 2006, Chs 1–2; Sandler, 2007, Ch. 2; Tropiani, 2009, pp. 90–7. The 1968 'Code of Self-Regulation' is reprinted in Steinberg, 1980, pp. 405–25; and Tropiani, 2009, pp. 291–3.

37 See Trevelyan, 1973; Phelps, 1975; Robertson, 1989, Ch. 4; Heins, 2001, Ch. 3; Aldgate and Robertson, 2005.

38 See the files on *Along Came a Spider* (submitted in 1953), *Natural Child* (1956), *The Burning Secret* (1956) and *Passion Flower Hotel* (1965) in the Production Code Administration collection at AMPAS. On the latter project, cp. LoBrutto, 1998, p. 229.

39 See the material in the so far uncatalogued 'Project Blue Movie' box, SKA. Cp. LoBrutto, 1998, pp. 329–30.

40 With its surprising reference to classical music, the tagline for *A Clockwork Orange* also echoes the opening lines of the film *Love Story* (and its bestselling source novel), the biggest hit of 1970: 'What can you say about a twenty-five-year-old girl who died? That she was beautiful. And brilliant. That she loved Mozart and Bach. And the Beatles. And me.'

41 Karlin, 1972. While there is no reason to doubt Karlin's comment on Kubrick, the filmmaker was disturbed by the fact that Karlin was required to report all of their conversations to Warner executive Norman Katz, finding 'this procedure odious and insulting. … I am not going to comment on any of these memos as to accuracy nor do I accept any responsibility for any views attributed to me' (Kubrick, 1972). On local authorities banning the film, see Phelps, 1975, pp. 168–9; and Robertson, 1989, p. 148.

42 This statement, together with the fact that the two films which, in effect, brought down the Production Code and ushered in the 'New Hollywood' (*Who's Afraid of Virginia Woolf?* and *Bonnie and Clyde*) had both been made by Warner Bros., and that the studio also released many violent crime movies and other controversial films in the late 1960s and early 1970s, would seem to suggest that perhaps there was a general studio policy at work here.

43 Cp. a study of the audience for 'X'-rated movies in 1973, which closely identifies such films with sexually explicit material. This study characterises the audience as consisting disproportionally of 'young single male[s] with at least a high-school education', without 'a particular religious affiliation', residing 'in a more populated area in the Eastern or Western regions of the United States', and notes that 'females attend X-rated films in lower percentages than males, and smaller percentages of the female attenders return in comparison to males' (Klenow and Crane, 1977, pp. 77–8).

44 The editorial was reprinted, together with a response from Stanley Kubrick, in the *New York Times*, 1972.

45 Canby had written an earlier review of the film, published in the *New York Times*, 20 December 1971, p. 44.

46 For a discussion of the political context from which such anxieties about American 'fascism' emerged, see, for example, Perlstein, 2009.

47 Broadly speaking, the audience for *A Clockwork Orange* thus seems to be very similar to that of 'X'-rated movies in general (cp. Klenow and Crane, 1977).

48 It is not altogether clear why 'inflaming' people to sex should be considered a bad thing, and also why, of all newspapers, it was the *Sun* complaining about pornography when it was the very paper that pushed the sexualisation of British tabloids.

49 Cp. Hall *et al.*, 1978; and Waddington, 1988. On reactions against 'permissiveness', see Sandbrook, 2007, Ch. 16; and Sandbrook, 2010, Ch. 11.

50 With regards to the US, see, for example, Yankelovich, 1974; Mayer, 1993; and Steinhorn, 2006. It is important to point out that the developments of the 1960s and 1970s are best understood as an intensification of earlier trends. So rather than seeing the 1950s as a period of stability or stasis, which is overcome by the cultural revolution of the 1960s, it is more appropriate to emphasise the profound changes American society was undergoing throughout the 1940s and 1950s, which prepared the ground for later transformations. Cp. Petigny, 2009. With regards to the UK, see, for example, Sandbrook, 2007, Ch. 16; and Sandbrook, 2010, Ch. 11. Once again the changes of the 1960s can be related to earlier developments. For discussions of such continuities – in society at large, in the conflict between pressure groups and in the sphere of culture, with a particular emphasis on the late 1950s – see, for example, Sandbrook, 2006; Pym, 1974; and Aldgate, 1995.

51 See Krämer, 2005, Chs 1–3; Powers, Rothman and Rothman, 1996; and Hunt, 1998, Chs 2–3, 6–8.

52 See Docherty, Morrison and Tracey, 1987, pp. 2–3, 29–30; and Hanson, 2007, p. 93. However, unlike in the US, attendance levels in the UK did not reach their lowest point until the early 1980s.

53 See Prince, 1998, 2000 and 2003, Ch. 6; Lewis, 2000, Chs 4–5; Williams, 2008, Chs 2–3; Hunt, 1998.

54 On general trends in American film criticism, see Taylor, 1999. esp. Chs 5–7; Haberski, 2001, Chs 7–10; Haberski, 2007, esp. pp. 177–230; Baumann, 2007. Haberski also references numerous British critics. On the critical reception of *A Clockwork Orange*, see Barr, 1972, for the UK; and Staiger, 2003, for the US.

55 Cp. for the US, Mayer, 1993, pp. 263–70; and, for the UK, Waddington, 1986; and Reiner, Livingstone and Allen, 2000.

56 See National Commission on the Causes and Prevention of Violence, 1970; Commission on Obscenity and Pornography, 1970; Glucksman, 1971, esp. pp. 68–78; Surgeon General's Scientific Advisory Committee on Television and Social Behavior, 1972; Longford Committee Investigating Pornography, 1972; Cline, 1974; Phelps, 1975, Ch. 10.

57 Elsaesser acknowledges the importance of Barr's work on p. 176.

58 For example, Walker, 1972c (an earlier version had been published in 1971 in the UK); Kagan, 1972; De Vries, 1973; Phillips, 1975; Nelson, 1982; Ciment, 1983 (the original French version had been published in 1980). The first scholarly guide to the growing literature on Kubrick appeared in 1980 (Coyne, 1980).

59 For example, Falsetto, 1994 and 1996; Jenkins, 1997; and Mainar, 1999.

60 For example, Walker, Taylor and Ruchti, 1999; Kagan, 2000; Nelson, 2000; Falsetto, 2001; and Ciment, 2001.

61 For example, Rasmussen, 2001; Cocks, 2004; Sperb, 2006; Naremore, 2007; and Rice, 2008.

62 For example, Cocks, Diedrick and Perusek, 2005; Abrams, 2007; and Rhodes, 2008. Also see the special issue of *Literature/Film Quarterly* (2001).

63 For example, Howard, 1999; Hughes, 2000; Phillips, 2001; Duncan, 2003; and Castle, 2005.

64 For example, Gehrke, 2001; McDougal, 2003; Winchell, 2008, Ch. 8; Aisenberg, 2008; and Eder, 2008.

65 For example, Hunt, 1998, Ch. 5; Chapman, 1999; Catterall and Wells, 2001, pp. 102–21; Buovolo, 2004; Ede, 2010, pp. 145–9; and Smith, 2010a.

66 For a discussion of the film's critical reception in the US, see Staiger, 2003.

67 For example, Trevelyan, 1973, esp. Ch. 15; and Phelps, 1975, esp. pp. 80–6 and 168–76.

68 For example, Robertson, 1989, pp. 143–9; and Petley, 1995.

69 For example, Cumberbatch, 2002; Barker and Mathijs, 2005; and Smith, 2010b.

70 The cover of Paul Newland's 2010 collection of essays on British cinema in the 1970s consists of graphics originally used in the marketing of *A Clockwork Orange*.

71 See the many clippings from 1974–6 contained in volume 6 of SK/13/6/30, SKA.

72 In the US, the film was released on video in 1980, and it received yet another theatrical release in 1982 (*Variety*, 1980; Warner Bros., 1982).

73 The name of the author is known to me but to protect her anonymity, I identify this particular letter with reference to its date and the correspondent's home town, here 27 March 1972, Columbus, OH, SK/13/8/6/18, SKA.

Appendix C: References

Abbreviations

AMPAS: Margaret Herrick Library, Academy of Motion Picture Arts and Sciences, Beverly Hills, CA.
BBFC: British Board of Film Classification, London.
CARA: Code and Rating Administration.
PARC: Performing Arts Research Center, New York Public Library, New York.
SKA: Stanley Kubrick Archive, University of the Arts London.

Abrams, Jerold J. (ed.) (2007) *The Philosophy of Stanley Kubrick*. Lexington: University Press of Kentucky.

Aggeler, Geoffrey (1979) *Anthony Burgess: The Artist as Novelist*. Tuscaloosa: University of Alabama Press.

Aisenberg, Joseph (2008) 'Counter Clockwise, or Lay Quiet Awhile with Ed and Id Molotov: Re-examining the Crossed Wires in Kubrick's and Burgess's *A Clockwork Orange*', *Bright Lights Film Journal* no. 61: http://www.brightlightsfilm.com/61/61clockwork.php.

Aldgate, Anthony (1995) *Censorship and the Permissive Society: British Cinema and Theatre, 1955–1965*. Oxford: Clarendon.

Aldgate, Anthony, and James C. Robertson (2005) *Censorship in Theatre and Cinema*. Edinburgh: Edinburgh University Press.

Allardyce Hampshire (1972) 'Schedule of Advertising/Entertainments Publicity Division', several documents dated from 18 July 1972 and 29 December 1972, SK/13/6/16, SKA.

Allen, Bill (1972) '*A Clockwork Orange* – Fascinatingly Tart or Merely Putrid?', *Pittsburgh Press*, 20 March.

Allison, Julie A. and Lawrence S. Wrightsman (1993) *Rape: The Misunderstood Crime*. London: Sage.

Analog (1963) Review of *A Clockwork Orange*, *Analog Science Fact Science Fiction*, unpaginated clipping in SK/13/6/29/45, SKA, p. 94.

Anderson, Craig (1985) *Science Fiction Films of the Seventies*. Jefferson, NC: McFarland.

Baptist Times (1972) 'Violence in the Cinema', 6 January, unpaginated clipping in SK/13/6/30, vol. 1, SKA.

Barker, Martin (1984a) *A Haunt of Fears: The Strange History of the British Horror Comics Campaign*. London: Pluto Press.

Barker, Martin (ed.) (1984b) *The Video Nasties*. London: Pluto Press.

Barker, Martin (2004) 'Violence Redux', in Steven Jay Schneider (ed.) *New Hollywood Violence*. Manchester: Manchester University Press, pp. 57–79.

Barker, Martin (2005) 'Loving and Hating *Straw Dogs*: The Meanings of Audience Responses to a Controversial Film', *Participations* vol. 2 no. 2, December: http://www.participations.org/volume2/issue2/2_02_barker.htm.

Barker, Martin (2006) 'Loving and Hating *Straw Dogs*: The Meanings of Audience Responses to a Controversial Film – Part 2: Rethinking *Straw Dogs*', *Participations* vol. 3 no. 1, May: http://www.participations.org/volume3/issue1/3_01_barker.htm.

Barker, Martin, Jane Arthurs and Ramaswami Harindranath (2001) *The Crash Controversy: Censorship Campaigns and Film Reception*. London: Wallflower Press.

Barker, Martin, and Kate Brooks (1998) *Knowing Audiences: Judge Dredd, Its Friends, Fans and Foes*. Luton: University of Luton Press.

Barker, Martin, and Ernest Mathijs (2005) 'Understanding Vernacular Experiences of Film in an Academic Environment', *Art, Design and Communication in Higher Education* vol. 4 no. 1, pp. 49–71.

Barker, Martin, and Julian Petley (eds) (1997) *Ill Effects: The Media/Violence Debate*. London: Routledge.

Barr, Charles (1972) '*Straw Dogs*, *A Clockwork Orange* and the Critics', *Screen* vol. 13 no. 2, Summer, pp. 17–31.

Barroch, Robert (1972) 'Pornography?', *Journal* (Newcastle upon Tyne), 18 January, unpaginated clipping in SK/13/6/30, vol. 1, SKA.

Baumann, Shyon (2007) *Hollywood Highbrow: From Entertainment to Art*. Princeton, NJ: Princeton University Press.

Baumeister, Roy F. (1996) *Evil: Inside Human Cruelty and Violence*. New York: W. H. Freeman.

Baxter, John (1998) *Stanley Kubrick: A Biography*. London: HarperCollins.

BBFC (1967) Letter to Richard Gregson, 2 June, file on *A Clockwork Orange*, BBFC.

Beaty, Bart (2005) *Fredric Wertham and the Critique of Mass Culture*. Jackson: University Press of Mississippi.

Berkeley Gazette (1963) Review of *A Clockwork Orange*, 26 January, unpaginated clipping in SK/13/6/29/45, SKA.

Best, Joel (ed.) (1989) *Images of Issues: Typifying Contemporary Social Problems*. New York: Aldine de Gruyter.

Best, Joel (1990) *Threatened Children: Rhetoric and Concern about Child-Victims*. Chicago, IL: University of Chicago Press.

Best, Joel (1999) *Random Violence: How We Talk about New Crimes and New Victims*. Berkeley: University of California Press.

Biderman, Albert D. (1962) 'The Image of "Brainwashing"', *Public Opinion Quarterly* vol. 26 no. 4, Winter, pp. 547–63.

Biltereyst, Daniel (2005) 'Youth, Moral Panics, and the End of Cinema: On the Reception of *Rebel without a Cause*', in J. David Slocum (ed.) *Rebel without a Cause: Approaches to a Maverick Masterwork*. Albany: State University of New York Press, pp. 171–89.

Biswell, Andrew (2005) *The Real Life of Anthony Burgess*. London: Picador.

Black, Gregory D. (1998) *The Catholic Crusade against the Movies, 1940–1975*. Cambridge: Cambridge University Press.

Blumenthal, Ralph (1972) 'Gang's Invasion of Home in Riverdale Spurs Plans for Security', *New York Times*, 21 January, p. 48.

Blyth, Jeffrey (1972) 'Hunt for *Clockwork Orange* Sex Gang', *Sunday People*, 23 January, unpaginated clipping in SK/13/6/30, vol. 1, SKA.

Boëthius, Ulf (1995) 'Youth, the Media and Moral Panics', in Johan Fornäs and Göran Bolin (eds) *Youth Culture in Late Modernity*. London: Sage, pp. 39–57.

Bok, Sissela (1999) *Mayhem: Violence as Public Entertainment*. Reading, MA: Perseus Books.

Boucher, Anthony (1963) 'Best Mysteries of the Month', *Ellery Queens Mystery Magazine*, April, unpaginated clipping in SK/13/6/29/45, SKA.

Bourke, Joanna (2008) *Rape: A History from 1860 to the Present*. London: Virago.

Brewer, Jeutonne (1980) *Anthony Burgess: A Bibliography*. Metuchen, NJ: Scarecrow Press.

Brown, Michelle (2009) *The Culture of Punishment: Prison, Society, and Spectacle*. New York: New York University Press.

Buckingham, David (1996) *Moving Images: Understanding Children's Emotional Responses to Television*. Manchester: Manchester University Press.

Buovolo, Marisa (2004) 'Masken der Gewalt: Die Sprache der Kleidung in *A Clockwork Orange*', *Kinematograph* no. 19, pp. 148–55.

Burden, Peter (1972) 'What Police Think of *The Clockwork Orange* [sic]', *Daily Mail*, 12 January, unpaginated clipping in SK/13/6/30, vol. 1, SKA.

Burgess, Anthony (1962/1972) *A Clockwork Orange*. London: Penguin. (This British version of the novel was first published by William Heinemann in 1962.)

Burgess, Anthony (1962) *The Wanting Seed*. London: Heinemann.

Burgess, Anthony (1969) '*A Clockwork Orange* First Draft Screenplay', SK/13/1/5, SKA. (The script is not dated, but it was written in 1969.)

Burgess, Anthony (1972) 'Author Has His Say on *Clockwork* Film', *Los Angeles Times*, 13 February, Calendar, pp. 1, 18–19.

Butsch, Richard (2008) *The Citizen Audience: Crowds, Publics, and Individuals*. New York: Routledge.

Cable, Michael (1971) 'Coming Shortly, a Film for None of the Family', *Daily Mail*, 30 December, unpaginated clipping in SK/13/6/30, vol. 1, SKA.

Cameron, Deborah, and Elizabeth Frazer (1987) *The Lust to Kill: A Feminist Investigation of Sexual Murder*. Cambridge: Polity Press.

Campbell, Anne, Steven Munce and John Galea (1982) 'American Gangs and British Subcultures: A Comparison', *International Journal of Offender Therapy and Comparative Criminology* vol. 26, pp. 76–89.

Canby, Vincent (1972) '*Orange* – "Disorienting But Human Comedy"…', *New York Times*, 9 January, Section 2, pp. 1, 7.

Caputi, Jane (1988) *The Age of Sex Crime*. London: Women's Press.

CARA (1971) MPAA Certificate of Approval for X-Rated Version of *A Clockwork Orange*, dated 15 December, SK/13/8/5/10, SKA.

CARA (1972) MPAA Certificate of Approval for R-rated Version of *A Clockwork Orange*, dated 22 August, SK/13/6/29/43/1, SKA.

Carruthers, Susan L. (1998) '*The Manchurian Candidate* (1962) and the Cold War Brainwashing Scare', *Historical Journal of Film, Radio and Television* vol. 18 no. 1, pp. 75–94.

Carruthers, Susan L. (2009) *Cold War Captives: Imprisonment, Escape, and Brainwashing*. Berkeley: University of California Press.

Cashin, Fergus (1972) 'Yeah, Reggie, You Must See This', *Sun*, 11 January, unpaginated clipping in SK/13/6/30, vol. 1, SKA.

Castle, Alison (ed.) (2005) *The Stanley Kubrick Archives*. Cologne: Taschen.

Castle, Alison (ed.) (2010) *Stanley Kubrick's* Napoleon*: The Greatest Movie Never Made*. London: Taschen. (This publication consists of several volumes.)

Catterall, Ali, and Simon Wells (2001) *Your Face Here: British Cult Movies since the Sixties*. London: Fourth Estate.

Chapman, James (1999) ' "A Bit of the Old Ultra-violence": *A Clockwork Orange*', in I. Q. Hunter (ed.) *British Science Fiction Cinema*. London: Routledge, pp. 128–37.

Chauncey, George, Jr. (1993) 'The Postwar Sex Crime Panic', in William Graebner (ed.) *True Stories from the American Past*. New York: McGraw-Hill, pp. 160–78.

Chibnall, Steve, and Robert Murphy (eds) (1999) *British Crime Cinema*. London: Routledge.

Christian Science Monitor (1971) Review of *A Clockwork Orange*, 20 December, p. 4.

Ciment, Michel (1983) *Kubrick*. London: Collins.

Ciment, Michel (2001) *Kubrick: The Definitive Edition*. London: Faber and Faber.

Clarke, John (1973) 'Football Hooliganism and the Skinheads', occasional paper, Centre for Contemporary Cultural Studies, University of Birmingham.

Cline, Victor B. (ed.) (1974) *Where Do You Draw the Line? An Exploration into Media Violence, Pornography, and Censorship*. Provo, UT: Brigham Young University Press.

Cocks, Geoffrey (2004) *The Wolf at the Door: Stanley Kubrick, History, and the Holocaust*. New York: Peter Lang.

Cocks, Geoffrey, James Diedrick and Glenn Perusek (eds) (2005) *Depth of Field: Stanley Kubrick, Film, and the Uses of History*. Madison: University of Wisconsin Press.

Cohan, Steven (1997) *Masked Men: Masculinity and the Movies in the Fifties*. Bloomington: Indiana University Press.

Cohen, Ronald D. (1997) '*The Delinquents*: Censorship and Youth Culture in Recent US History', *History of Education Quarterly* vol. 37 no. 3, Fall, pp. 251–70.

Cohen, Stanley (1972/2002) *Folk Devils and Moral Panics: The Creation of the Mods and Rockers*, 3rd edn. London: Routledge. (The first edition was published in 1972.)

Cole, Phillip (2008) *The Myth of Evil*. Edinburgh: Edinburgh University Press.

Commission on Obscenity and Pornography (1970) *Report of the Commission on Obscenity and Pornography*. New York: Bantam.

Considine, David M. (1985) *The Cinema of Adolescence*. Jefferson, NC: McFarland.

Coyle, Wallace (1980) *Stanley Kubrick: A Guide to References and Resources*. Boston, MA: G. K. Hall.

Critcher, Chas (2003) *Moral Panics and the Media*. Buckingham: Open University Press.

Cumberbatch, Guy (2002) *Where Do You Draw the Line? Attitudes and Reactions of Video Renters to Sexual Violence in Film*. Birmingham: Communications Research Group, http://www.bbfc.co.uk/download/policy-and-research/Where do you draw the line.pdf.

Daily Telegraph (1973) 'Gallup Poll: *Crossroads* Is Top TV Programme', 22 December, unpaginated clipping in SK/13/6/30, vol. 5, SKA.

Daily Telegraph (2010) ' "Homophobic" Killing: Teenage Girls Attacked Man Like a Scene from *Clockwork Orange*, Jury Told', 20 April, p. 4.

Daily Variety (1972) 'Kubrick Subs 30 Seconds of Film and *Clockwork* Sheds X, Gets R', 25 August, pp. 1, 8.

Daily Variety (1974) '*Clockwork Orange* London Perennial, Now in Third Year', 11 January, p. 1.

Daniels, Don (1972/73) '*A Clockwork Orange*', *Sight and Sound*, Winter, pp. 44–6.

DeVitis, A. A. (1972) *Anthony Burgess*. New York: Twayne.

De Vries, Daniel (1973) *The Films of Stanley Kubrick*. Grand Rapids, MI: Eerdmans Publishing.

Dickinson, Margaret, and Sarah Street (1985) *Cinema and State: The Film Industry and the British Government, 1927–84*. London: BFI.

Disc (1974) 'Top Film', 16 February, unpaginated clipping in SK/13/6/30, vol. 5, SKA.

Docherty, David, David Morrison and Michael Tracey (1987) *The Last Picture Show? Britain's Changing Film Audiences*. London: BFI.

Doherty, Thomas (1988) *Teenagers and Teenpics: The Juvenilization of American Movies in the 1950s*. Boston, MA: Unwin Hyman.

Doherty, Thomas (2007) *Hollywood's Censor: Joseph I. Breen and the Production Code Administration*. New York: Columbia University Press.

Donovan, Barna William (2010) *Blood, Guns, and Testosterone: Action Films, Audiences, and a Thirst for Violence*. Lanham, MD: Scarecrow Press.

Douglass, Wayne J. (1981) 'The Criminal Psychopath as Hollywood Hero', *Journal of Popular Film and Television* vol. 8 no. 4, pp. 30–9.

Downes, David (1966) *The Delinquent Solution*. London: Routledge and Kegan Paul.

Duncan, Paul (2003) *Stanley Kubrick: Visual Poet 1928–1999*. Cologne: Taschen.

Ede, Laurie N. (2010) *British Film Design: A History*. London: I. B. Tauris.

Edelman, Maurice (1972) 'Clockwork Oranges Are Ticking Bombs', *Evening News* (London), 27 January, unpaginated clipping in SK/13/6/30, vol. 1, SKA.

Eder, Jens (2008) 'Feelings in Conflict: *A Clockwork Orange* and the Explanation of Audiovisual Emotions', *Projections* vol. 2 no. 2, Winter, pp. 66–84.

Edwards, Anne (1972) 'What Good Can This Film Possibly Do?', *Sunday Express*, 16 January, unpaginated clipping in SK/13/6/30, vol. 1, SKA.

Egan, Kate (2007) *Trash or Treasure? Censorship and the Changing Meaning of the Video Nasties*. Manchester: Manchester University Press.

Ehrenreich, Barbara (1983) *The Hearts of Men: American Dreams and the Flight from Commitment*. London: Pluto Press.

Elsaesser, Thomas (1976) 'Screen Violence: Emotional Structure and Ideological Function in *A Clockwork Orange*', in C. W. E. Bigsby (ed.) *Approaches to Popular Culture*. London: Edward Arnold, pp. 171–200.

Eriksson, Georg (Warner Bros.) (1976) Letter to Stanley Kubrick, 16 January, SK/13/5/25, SKA.

Evans, Walter (1974) 'Violence and Film: The Thesis of Kubrick's *A Clockwork Orange*', *The Velvet Light Trap* no. 13, Fall, pp. 11–12.

Falkirk Herald (1973) 'A Bizarre Cult – or a New Fashion Fad?', 31 March, unpaginated clipping in SK/13/6/30, vol. 4, SKA.

Falsetto, Mario (1994) *Stanley Kubrick: A Narrative and Stylistic Analysis*. Westport, CT: Greenwood Press.

Falsetto, Mario (ed.) (1996) *Perspectives on Stanley Kubrick*. Boston, MA: G. K. Hall.

Falsetto, Mario (2001) *Stanley Kubrick: A Narrative and Stylistic Analysis. New and Expanded Second Edition*. Westport, CT: Praeger.

Farber, Stephen (1972) *The Movie Rating Game*. Washington, DC: Public Affairs Press.

Farber, Stephen, and Estelle Changas (1972) 'Putting the Hex on "R" and "X" ', *New York Times*, 9 April, p. D1.

Films and Filming (1973) 'Box Office Champions', *Films and Filming*, January, unpaginated clipping in SK/13/6/30, vol. 3, SKA.

Films Illustrated (1973) 'Films of the Year', January, unpaginated clipping in SK/13/6/30, vol. 3, SKA.

Finler, Joel W. (2003) *The Hollywood Story*. London: Wallflower Press.

Fowler, David (2008) *Youth Culture in Modern Britain, c. 1920 – c. 1970: From Ivory Tower to Global Movement – A New History*. Basingstoke: Palgrave.

Freedman, Estelle B. (1987) 'Responses to the Sexual Psychopath, 1920–1960', *Journal of American History* vol. 74 no. 1, June, pp. 83–106.

Fyvel, T. R. (1963/1997) 'Fashion and Revolt', extract from the revised edition of *The Insecure Offenders: Rebellious Youth in the Welfare State*. London: Penguin, reprinted in Ken Gelder and Sarah Thornton (eds) *The Subcultures Reader*. London: Routledge, pp. 388–92.

Gehrke, Pat J. (2001) 'Deviant Subjects in Foucault and *A Clockwork Orange*: Congruent Critiques of Criminological Constructions of Subjectivity', *Critical Studies in Mass Communication* vol. 18 no. 2, September, pp. 270–84.

Gelder, Ken, and Sarah Thornton (eds) (1997) *The Subcultures Reader*. London: Routledge.

Gelmis, Joseph (1970/2001) 'The Film Director as Superstar: Stanley Kubrick', in Gene D. Phillips (ed.) *Stanley Kubrick: Interviews*. Jackson: University Press of Mississippi, pp. 81–104. (Originally published in Joseph Gelmis [1970] *The Film Director as Superstar*. New York: Doubleday, pp. 293–316.)

Gelmis, Joseph (1972) 'Kubrick Tells Why of *Clockwork* Film', *Courier Journal and Times*, 8 October, p. H2.

Gibbs, Patrick (1972) 'America Puts on New Clothes', *Daily Telegraph*, 29 December, unpaginated clipping in SK/13/6/30, vol. 3, SKA.

Gilbert, Basil (1974) 'Kubrick's Marmalade: The Art of Violence', *Meanjin Quarterly*, Winter, pp. 157–62.

Gilbert, James (1986) *A Cycle of Outrage: America's Reaction to the Juvenile Delinquent in the 1950s*. New York: Oxford University Press.

Gilbert Youth Research (1972) 'Theater Survey on *A Clockwork Orange*', report submitted to Warner Bros. in March in SK/13/5/7, SKA.

Gilligan, James (2000) *Violence: Reflections on Our Deadliest Epidemic*. London: Jessica Kingsley Publishers.

Glucksmann, André (1971) *Violence on the Screen: A Report on Research into the Effects on Young People of Scenes of Violence in Films and Television*. London: BFI Education Department.

Godfrey, Derek (1973) 'Mugging Murder in Church Porch', *Evening News* (London), 5 April, unpaginated clipping in SK/13/6/30, vol. 4, SKA.

Goldstein, Jeffrey H. (1998) 'Why We Watch', in Jeffrey H. Goldstein (ed.) *Why We Watch: The Attractions of Violent Entertainment*. New York: Oxford University Press, pp. 212–26.

Goode, Erich, and Nachman Ben-Yehuda (1994) *Moral Panics: The Social Construction of Deviance*. Oxford: Blackwell.

Gottfredson, Michael R., and Travis Hirschi (1990) *A General Theory of Crime*. Stanford, CA: Stanford University Press.

Greenberg, Gary (2011) *Manufacturing Depression: The Secret History of a Modern Disease*. London: Bloomsbury.

Grieveson, Lee (2008) 'Cinema Studies and the Conduct of Conduct', in Lee Grieveson and Haidee Wasson (eds) *Inventing Film Studies*. Durham, NC: Duke University Press, pp. 3–37.

Gumenik, Arthur (1972) '*A Clockwork Orange*: Novel into Film', *Film Heritage* vol. 7 no. 4, Summer, pp. 7–18.

Haberski, Raymond J., Jr (2001) *It's Only a Movie! Films and Critics in American Culture*. Lexington: University Press of Kentucky.

Haberski, Raymond J., Jr (2007) *Freedom to Offend: How New York Remade Movie Culture*. Lexington: University Press of Kentucky.

Hall, Sheldon (1999) *Hard Ticket Giants: Hollywood Blockbusters in the Widescreen Era* (two volumes), unpublished PhD dissertation, University of East Anglia.

Hall, Stuart, Chas Critcher, Tony Jefferson, John Clarke and Brian Roberts (1978) *Policing the Crisis: Mugging, the State, and Law and Order*. Basingstoke: Macmillan.

Hall, William (1972) '*Clockwork Orange* Gang Killed My Wife', *Evening News* (London), 28 January, p. 10.

Hanson, Stuart (2007) *From Silent Screen to Multi-Screen: A History of Cinema Exhibition in Britain since 1896*. Manchester: Manchester University Press.

Harris, Mai (1972) '*A Clockwork Orange* Release Script', dated March, SK/13/1/13–14, SKA.

Harris, Mark (2009) *Scenes from a Revolution: The Birth of the New Hollywood*. Edinburgh: Canongate.

Hebdige, Dick (1979) *Subculture: The Meaning of Style*. London: Routledge.

Hebdige, Dick (1988) *Hiding in the Light: On Images and Things*. London: Comedia.

Hechinger, Fred M. (1972) 'A Liberal Fights Back', *New York Times*, 13 February, Section 2, pp. 1, 33.

Heins, Marjorie (2001) *Not in Front of the Children: 'Indecency', Censorship, and the Innocence of Youth*. New York: Hill and Wang.

Hill, Annette (1997) *Shocking Entertainment: Viewer Response to Violent Movies*. Luton: John Libbey Media.

Hill, James (1972) 'Brutal Film Shocked Me', *Southern Evening Echo* (Southampton), 14 February, unpaginated clipping in SK/13/6/30, vol. 2, SKA.

Hill, Lee (2001) *A Grand Guy: The Art and Life of Terry Southern*. London: Bloomsbury.

Hine, Thomas (1999) *The Rise and Fall of the American Teenager*. New York: Avon.

Hoberman, J. (1998) ' "A Test for the Individual Viewer": *Bonnie and Clyde*'s Violent Reception', in Jeffrey H. Goldstein (ed.) *Why We Watch: The Attractions of Violent Entertainment*. New York: Oxford University Press, pp. 116–43.

Hofsess, John (1971/2001) 'Mind's Eye: *A Clockwork Orange*', *Take One*, May–June 1971, reprinted in Gene D. Phillips (ed.) *Stanley Kubrick: Interviews*. Jackson: University Press of Mississippi, pp. 105–7.

Hoggart, Richard (1957) *The Uses of Literacy*. London: Chatto and Windus.

Hollywood Reporter (1972) '*Clockwork Orange* Is Setting Records', 23 March, unpaginated clipping on the *Clockwork Orange* fiche, AMPAS.

Houston, Penelope (1971/2001) 'Kubrick Country', *Saturday Review*, 25 December 1971, reprinted in Gene D. Phillips (ed.) *Stanley Kubrick: Interviews*. Jackson: University Press of Mississippi, pp. 108–15.

Howard, James (1999) *Stanley Kubrick Companion*. London: Batsford Books.

Hughes, David (2000) *The Complete Kubrick*. London: Virgin.

Hunt, Leon (1998) *British Low Culture: From Safari Suits to Sexploitation*. London: Routledge.

Hunter, I. Q. (1999) *British Science Fiction Cinema*. London: Routledge.

Huxley, Aldous (1932/2007) *Brave New World*. London: Vintage.

Hyman, Stanley Edgar (1963) 'Anthony Burgess: Clockwork Oranges', *New Leader*, 7 January, pp. 22–3.

Ingham, Robert, *et al.* (1978) *'Football Hooliganism': The Wider Context*. London: Inter-Action Imprint.

Isaac, Neil D. (1973) 'Unstuck in Time: *Clockwork Orange* and *Slaughterhouse Five*', *Literature/Film Quarterly* vol. 1 no. 2, Spring, pp. 122–31.

Jacobson, Matthew Frye, and Gaspar Gonzalez (2006) *What Have They Built You to Do? The Manchurian Candidate and Cold War America*. Minneapolis: University of Minnesota Press.

Jefferson, Tony (1975/1993) 'Cultural Responses of the Teds', in Stuart Hall and Tony Jefferson (eds) *Resistance through Rituals: Youth Subcultures in Post-War Britain*, 2nd edn. London: Routledge, pp. 67–70. (This book was originally published in 1975.)

Jenkins, Greg (1997) *Stanley Kubrick and the Art of Adaptation*. Jefferson, NC: McFarland.

Jenkins, Philip (1992) *Intimate Enemies: Moral Panics in Contemporary Great Britain*. New York: Aldine de Gruyter.

Jenkins, Philip (1994) *Using Murder: The Social Construction of Serial Homicide*. New York: Aldine de Gruyter.

Jenkins, Philip (1998) *Moral Panic: Changing Concepts of the Child Molester in Modern America*. New Haven, CT: Yale University Press.

Jones, Gerard (2002) *Killing Monsters: Why Children Need Fantasy, Super Heroes, and Make-Believe Violence*. New York: Basic Books.

Jowett, Garth (1976) *Film: The Democratic Art*. Boston, MA: Little, Brown.

Kagan, Norman (1972) *The Cinema of Stanley Kubrick*. New York: Holt, Rinehart and Winston.

Kagan, Norman (2000) *The Cinema of Stanley Kubrick*, 3rd edn. Oxford: Roundhouse.

Karlin, Myron D. (1972) Memo to Norman B. Katz, 9 February, SK/13/8/3/45, SKA.

Kekes, John (2005) *The Roots of Evil*. Ithaca, NY: Cornell University Press.

Kerr, John H. (1994) *Understanding Soccer Hooliganism*. Buckingham: Open University Press.

Klenow, Daniel J., and Jeffrey L. Crane (1977) 'Selected Characteristics of the X-rated Movie Audience: Toward a National Profile of the Recidivist', *Sociological Symposium* vol. 20, pp. 73–83.

Koch, Stephen (1991) *Stargazer*. New York: Marion Boyars.

Krämer, Peter (1999) 'A Powerful Cinema-going Force? Hollywood and Female Audiences since the 1960s', in Melvyn Stokes and Richard Maltby (eds) *Identifying Hollywood's Audiences: Cultural Identity and the Movies*. London: BFI, pp. 93–108.

Krämer, Peter (2005) *The New Hollywood: From* Bonnie and Clyde *to* Star Wars. London: Wallflower Press.

Krämer, Peter (2010a) '*A Clockwork Orange* (1971) and American Culture', unpublished paper presented at the Zentrum für Zeithistorische Forschung (Centre of Contemporary History), Potsdam, April.

Krämer, Peter (2010b) *2001: A Space Odyssey* (BFI Film Classics). London: BFI.

Krämer, Peter (2011) ' "Movies That Make People Sick": Audience Responses to Stanley Kubrick's *A Clockwork Orange* in 1971/72', unpublished paper presented at Aberystwyth University, May.

Krämer, Peter (forthcoming a) ' "Rape, Ultra-Violence and Beethoven": The Transgressiveness and Controversial Success of *A Clockwork Orange* (1971)', in Jacqui

Miller (ed.) *'What Would You Have Done?': Explorations of Ethics in Film Studies*. Liverpool: Liverpool Hope University Press.

Krämer, Peter (forthcoming b) 'The Limits of Autonomy: Stanley Kubrick, Hollywood and Independent Filmmaking, 1950–53', in Yannis Tzioumakis, Claire Molloy and Geoff King (eds) *American Independent Cinema*. London: Routledge.

Kubrick, Christiane (ed.) (2002) *Stanley Kubrick: A Life in Pictures*. London: Little, Brown.

Kubrick, Stanley (1969/2010) '*Napoleon*: A Screenplay', dated 29 September 1969, separate volume in Alison Castle (ed.) *Stanley Kubrick's* Napoleon: *The Greatest Movie Never Made*. London: Taschen.

Kubrick, Stanley (1970a) '*A Clockwork Orange*', screenplay dated 28 February, SK/13/1/10, SKA.

Kubrick, Stanley (1970b) '*A Clockwork Orange* Shooting Script', dated 7 September, SK/13/1/13, SKA.

Kubrick, Stanley (1971) '*A Clockwork Orange*: Stanley Kubrick Memorandum on Screenplays', dated 18 August, SK/13/8/5/10, SKA.

Kubrick, Stanley (1972/2000) *Stanley Kubrick's A Clockwork Orange. Based on the Novel by Anthony Burgess*. Southwold: Screenpress. (Originally published by Ballantine in 1972.)

Kubrick, Stanley (1972) Letter to Norman B. Katz, 10 February, SK/13/8/3/45, SKA.

Kubrick, Stanley (1976) Letter to Tom Nicholas at Columbia-Warner, 10 January, SK/13/5/25, SKA.

LA Herald Examiner (1971) 'Kubrick Sets *Traumnovelle*', 11 May, unpaginated clipping on Stanley Kubrick fiche, AMPAS.

Leff, Leonard J. (1998) 'A Test of American Film Censorship: *Who's Afraid of Virginia Woolf?* (1966)', in Peter C. Rollins (ed.) *Hollywood as Historian: American Film in a Cultural Context*, rev. edn. Lexington: University of Kentucky Press, pp. 211–29.

Leff, Leonard J., and Jerold L. Simmons (1990) *The Dame in the Kimono: Hollywood, Censorship, and the Production Code from the 1920s to the 1960s*. New York: Grove Weidenfeld.

Leitch, Thomas (2002) *Crime Films*. Cambridge: Cambridge University Press.

Leland, John (2004) *Hip: The History*. New York: Ecco.

Lewin, David (1972) 'Sex, Ultra Violence, Beethoven and Stanley Kubrick', *CinemaTV Today*, 15 January, p. 8.

Lewis, Jon (2000) *Hollywood v. Hardcore: How the Struggle over Censorship Saved the Modern Film Industry*. New York: New York University Press.

Lewis, Roger (2002) *Anthony Burgess*. London: Faber and Faber.

Lewis, Roger (2009) *Seasonal Suicide Notes: My Life as It Is Lived*. London: Short Books.

Leyton, Elliott (1986) *Hunting Humans: The Rise of the Modern Multiple Murderer*. London: Penguin.

Lindner, Robert M. (1944/2001) *Rebel without a Cause: The Story of a Criminal Psychopath*. New York: Other Press. (Originally published in 1944.)

Lister, David (1999) '*Clockwork Orange* Returns to British Screens', *Independent*, 2 December, p. 1.

Literature/Film Quarterly (2001), Special issue on Stanley Kubrick, vol. 29 no. 4.

Litman, Lenny (1972) 'Pittsburgh Editor Rebukes Critic, Sees *Clockwork* as Fatal Diagnosis', *Variety*, 29 March, unpaginated clipping in *Clockwork Orange* folder, AMPAS.

Litvinoff, Si (1970) Letter to Stanley Kubrick, 9 February, SK/13/8/5/12, SKA.

LoBrutto, Vincent (1998) *Stanley Kubrick*. London: Faber and Faber.

Londale, James (1993) 'Cinema Breached Kubrick Copyright', *The Times*, 24 March, p. 5.

Longford Committee Investigating Pornography (1972) *Pornography: The Longford Report*. London: Coronet.

Maguire, Mike (2002) 'Crime Statistics: The "Data Explosion" and Its Implications', in Mike Maguire, Rod Morgan and Robert Reiner (eds) *The Oxford Handbook of Criminology*, 3rd edn. Oxford: Oxford University Press, pp. 322–75.

Mailer, Norman (1957/1961) 'The White Negro: Superficial Reflections on the Hipster', *Dissent*, Summer 1957, reprinted in Norman Mailer (1961) *Advertisement for Myself*. London: Andre Deutsch, pp. 281–302.

Mainar, Luis M. Garcia (1999) *Narrative and Stylistic Patterns in the Films of Stanley Kubrick*. Rochester, NY: Camden House.

Malcolm, Derek (1972) untitled article, *Guardian*, 28 December, unpaginated clipping in SK/13/6/30, vol. 3, SKA.

Marwick, Arthur (1998) *The Sixties: Cultural Revolution in Britain, France, Italy, and the United States, c.1958–c.1974*. Oxford: Oxford University Press.

Mayer, William G. (1993) *The Changing American Mind: How and Why American Public Opinion Changed between 1960 and 1988*. Ann Arbor: University of Michigan Press.

McCann, Graham (1991) *Rebel Males: Clift, Brando and Dean*. London: Hamish Hamilton.

McCann, Paul (1999) 'Why Kubrick Lifted His *Clockwork Orange* Ban', *The Times*, 7 December, p. 9.

McDougal, Stuart Y. (ed.) (2003) *Stanley Kubrick's* A Clockwork Orange. Cambridge: Cambridge University Press.

McGeady, Paul J. (1974) 'Obscenity Law and the Supreme Court', in Victor B. Cline (ed.) *Where Do You Draw the Line? An Exploration into Media Violence, Pornography, and Censorship*. Provo, UT: Brigham Young University Press, pp. 83–106.

McGee, Mark Thomas, and R. J. Robertson (1982) *The J. D. Films: Juvenile Delinquency in the Movies*. Jefferson, NC: McFarland.

McGregor, Craig (1972) 'Nice Boy from the Bronx?', *New York Times*, 30 January, pp. 1, 13.

MacMillan, James (1972) 'Counterattack: Let's Put the Sex Pedlars [sic] out of Business', *Daily Express*, 18 January, unpaginated clipping in SK/13/6/30, vol. 1, SKA.

McQuiston, Kate (2008) 'Value, Violence, and Music Recognized: *A Clockwork Orange* as Musicology', in Gary D. Rhodes (ed.) *Stanley Kubrick: Essays on His Films and Legacy*. Jefferson, NC: McFarland, pp. 105–22.

Mishkin, Leo (1971) Review of *A Clockwork Orange*, *Morning Telegraph* (New York), 20 December, p. 3.

Moran, J. F. (1963) Review of *A Clockwork Orange*, *Library Journal*, 15 February, p. 793.

Morris, Robert K. (1971) *The Consolations of Ambiguity: An Essay on the Novels of Anthony Burgess*. Columbia: University of Missouri Press.

Morrison, David E. (1999) *Defining Violence: The Search for Understanding*. Luton: University of Luton Press.

Moskowitz, Kenneth (1976) '*A Clockwork Orange*', *The Velvet Light Trap* no. 16, pp. 28–31.

Moskowitz, Ken (1976/77) 'Clockwork Violence', *Sight and Sound*, Winter, pp. 22–4, 44.

Murdock, Graham (1997) 'Reservoirs of Dogma: An Archaeology of Popular Anxieties', in Martin Barker and Julian Petley (eds) *Ill Effects: The Media/Violence Debate*. London: Routledge, pp. 67–86.

Murphy, A. D. (1971) Review of *A Clockwork Orange*, *Variety*, 15 December, p. 14.

Murphy, Robert (1992) *Sixties British Cinema*. London: BFI.

Naremore, James (2007) *On Kubrick*. London: BFI.

National Commission on the Causes and Prevention of Violence (1970) *To Establish Justice, to Ensure Domestic Tranquility: The Final Report of the National Commission on the Causes and Prevention of Violence*. Washington, DC: US Government Printing Office.

Nelson, Thomas Allen (1982) *Kubrick: Inside a Film Artist's Maze*. Bloomington: Indiana University Press.

Nelson, Thomas Allen (2000) *Kubrick: Inside a Film Artist's Maze* (new and expanded edition). Bloomington: Indiana University Press.

New York Post (2001) 'Brits Finally Get *Clockwork*', 18 June, p. 86.

New York Times (1967) 'Clockwork Orange', 2 April, unpaginated clipping in the Si Litvinoff folder, PARC.

New York Times (1972) 'A Newspaper Says No to *Orange*', 23 April, pp. 11, 25.

Newland, Paul (ed.) (2010) *Don't Look Now: British Cinema in the 1970s*. Bristol: Intellect.

Newspaper Advertising Bureau (1974) 'Movie Going and Leisure Time', January; report contained in folder MFL x n.c. 2,101 no. 4, PARC.

Ornstein, Bill (1968) 'Litvinoff in 7-Feature Deal with Wagner', *Hollywood Reporter*, 1 February, unpaginated clipping in the Si Litvinoff folder, AMPAS.

Orwell, George (1949/1954) *Nineteen Eighty-Four*. London: Penguin. (First published in 1949.)

Osgerby, Bill (1998) *Youth in Britain since 1945*. Oxford: Blackwell.

O'Sullivan, Tom (2000) 'Going Like Clockwork', *Screen International*, 24 March, unpaginated clipping in the *Clockwork Orange* folder, AMPAS.

Palladino, Grace (1996) *Teenagers: An American History*. New York: Basic Books.

Parsons, Tony (1996) 'Alex through the Looking Glass', in Karl French (ed.) *Screen Violence*. London: Bloomsbury, pp. 179–85.

Pearson, Geoffrey (1983) *Hooligan: A History of Respectable Fears*. Basingstoke: Macmillan Education.

Pearson, Geoffrey (1984) 'Falling Standards: A Short, Sharp History of Moral Decline', in Martin Barker (ed.) *The Video Nasties: Freedom and Censorship in the Media*. London: Pluto Press, pp. 88–103.

Perlstein, Rick (2009) *Nixonland: The Rise of a President and the Fracturing of America*. New York: Scribner.

Petigny, Alan (2009) *The Permissive Society: America, 1941–1965*. Cambridge: Cambridge University Press.

Petley, Julian (1995) 'Clockwork Crimes: Chronicle of a Cause Célèbre', *Index on Censorship* vol. 24 no. 6, pp. 48–52.

Phelps, Guy (1975) *Film Censorship*. London: Victor Gollancz.

Phillips, Gene D. (1975) *Stanley Kubrick: A Film Odyssey*. New York: Popular Library.

Phillips, Gene D. (ed.) (2001) *Stanley Kubrick: Interviews*. Jackson: University Press of Mississippi.

Phillips, Gene D., and Rodney Hill (eds) (2002) *The Encyclopedia of Stanley Kubrick*. New York: Checkmark Books.

Plowright, Molly (1974) '*Orange* and Lemmon: Film Round-up for 1973', *Glasgow Herald*, 9 January, unpaginated clipping in SK/13/6/30, vol. 5, SKA.

Potter, W. James (1999) *On Media Violence*.Thousand Oaks, CA: Sage.

Powers, Stephen, David J. Rothman and Stanley Rothman (1996) *Hollywood's America: Social and Political Themes in Motion Pictures*. Boulder, CO: Westview Press.

Prince, Stephen (1998) *Savage Cinema: Sam Peckinpah and the Rise of Ultraviolent Movies*. London: Athlone Press.

Prince, Stephen (ed.) (2000) *Screening Violence*. New Brunswick, NJ: Rutgers University Press.

Prince, Stephen (2003) *Classical Film Violence: Designing and Regulating Brutality in Hollywood Cinema, 1930–1968*. New Brunswick, NJ: Rutgers University Press.

Pym, Bridget (1974) *Pressure Groups and the Permissive Society*. Newton Abbot: David and Charles.

Querry, Ronald B. (1973) 'Prison Movies: An Annotated Filmography 1921–Present', *Journal of Popular Film* vol. 2 no. 2, pp. 181–97.

Rabinowitz, Peter J. (2003) ' "A Bird Like Rarest Spun Heavenmetal": Music in *A Clockwork Orange*', in Stuart Y. McDougal (ed.) *Stanley Kubrick's* A Clockwork Orange. Cambridge: Cambridge University Press, pp. 109–30.

Rafter, Nicole (2000) *Shots in the Mirror: Crime Films and Society*. Oxford: Oxford University Press.

Rasmussen, Randy (2001) *Stanley Kubrick: Seven Films Analyzed*. Jefferson, NC: McFarland.

Record Mirror (1972) Review of *A Clockwork Orange*, 22 January, unpaginated clipping in SK/13/6/30, vol. 1, SKA

Reed, Rex (1971) Review of *A Clockwork Orange*, *New York Sunday News*, 26 December, p. 9.

Register Magazine (1963) 'Book to Read Oddy Knocky', 17 February, p. 6.

Reiner, Robert, Sonia Livingstone and Jessica Allen (2000) 'No More Happy Endings? The Media and Popular Concern about Crime since the Second World War', in Tim Hope and Richard Sparks (eds) *Crime, Risk and Insecurity*. London: Routledge, pp. 107–25.

Rhodes, Gary D. (ed.) (2008) *Stanley Kubrick: Essays on His Films and Legacy*. Jefferson, NC: McFarland.

Rhodes, Richard (1999) *Why They Kill: The Discoveries of a Maverick Criminologist*. New York: Alfred A. Knopf.

Rice, Julian (2008) *Kubrick's Hope: Discovering Optimism from* 2001 *to* Eyes Wide Shut. Lanham, MD: Scarecrow Press.

Riley, Clayton (1972) '… Or "A Dangerous, Criminally Irresponsible Horror Show" ', *New York Times*, 9 January, Section 2, pp. 1, 13.

Robertson, James C. (1989) *The Hidden Cinema: British Film Censorship in Action, 1913–1972*. London: Routledge.

Robinson, David (1972) 'Looking Back, Looking In', *Financial Times*, 29 December, unpaginated clipping in SK/13/6/30, vol. 3, SKA.

Rock, Paul, and Stanley Cohen (1970) 'The Teddy Boy', in Vernon Bogdanov and Robert Skidelsky (eds) *The Age of Affluence, 1951–1964*. London: Macmillan, pp. 288–320.

Roleston, Peter (1973) 'This Orange Is Certainly a Tangy Fruit', *Hereford Evening News*, 20 February, unpaginated clipping in SK/13/6/30, vol. 2, SKA.

Rubin, Martin (1992) 'The Grayness of Darkness: *The Honeymoon Killers* and Its Impact on Psychokiller Cinema', *The Velvet Light Trap* no. 30, Fall, pp. 48–64.

Rubin, Martin (1994) 'Make Love Make War: Cultural Confusion and the Biker Film Cycle', *Film History* vol. 6, pp. 355–81.

Sandbrook, Dominic (2006) *Never Had It So Good: A History of Britain from Suez to the Beatles*. London: Abacus Books.

Sandbrook, Dominic (2007) *White Heat: A History of Britain in the Swinging Sixties*. London: Abacus Books.

Sandbrook, Dominic (2010) *State of Emergency: The Way We Were: Britain, 1970–1974*. London: Allen Lane.

Sandler, Kevin (2007) *The Naked Truth: Why Hollywood Doesn't Make X-Rated Movies*. New Brunswick, NJ: Rutgers University Press.

Sarris, Andrew (1971) Review of *A Clockwork Orange*, *Village Voice*, 30 December, p. 49.

Savage, Jon (2008) *Teenage: The Creation of Youth 1875–1945*. London: Pimlico.

Schneider, Eric C. (1999) *Vampires, Dragon, and Egyptian Kings: Youth Gangs in Postwar New York*. Princeton, NJ: Princeton University Press.

Scott, Peter (1956/57) 'Gangs and Delinquent Groups in London', *British Journal of Delinquency* vol. 7, pp. 4–26.

Shaw, Daniel (2007) 'Nihilism and Freedom in the Films of Stanley Kubrick', in Jerold J. Abrams (ed.) *The Philosophy of Stanley Kubrick*. Lexington: University Press of Kentucky, pp. 221–34.

Simkin, Stevie (2011) *Straw Dogs*. London: Palgrave.

Simpson, Robert J. E. (2008) 'Whose Stanley Kubrick? The Myth, Legacy, and Ownership of the Kubrick Image', in Gary D. Rhodes (ed.) *Stanley Kubrick: Essays on His Films and Legacy*. Jefferson, NC: McFarland, pp. 232–44.

Siskel, Gene (1972/2001) 'Kubrick's Creative Concern', *Chicago Tribune*, 13 February 1972, reprinted in Gene D. Phillips (ed.) *Stanley Kubrick: Interviews*. Jackson: University Press of Mississippi, pp. 116–25.

Sklar, Robert (1988) 'Stanley Kubrick and the American Film Industry', *Current Research in Film* vol. 4, 1988, pp. 114–24.

Smith, Justin (2010a) 'The "Lack" and How to Get It: Reading Male Anxiety in *A Clockwork Orange*, *Tommy* and *The Man Who Fell to Earth*', in Paul Newland (ed.) *Don't Look Now: British Cinema in the 1970s*. Bristol: Intellect, pp. 143–60.

Smith, Justin (2010b) *Withnail and Us: Cult Film and Film Cults in British Cinema*. London: I. B. Tauris.

Sobchak, Thomas (1982) 'New York Street Gangs or the Warriors of My Mind', *Journal of Popular Film and Television* vol. 10 no. 2, Summer, pp. 77–85.

Sobchak, Vivian (1987) *Screening Space: The American Science Fiction Film*. New Brunswick, NJ: Rutgers University Press, 1987.

Soothill, Keith, and Sylvia Walby (1991) *Sex Crime in the News*. London: Routledge.

Sorlin, Sandrine (2009) '*A Clockwork Orange*: A Linguistic Symphony', in Marc Jeannin (ed.) *Anthony Burgess: Music in Literature and Literature in Music*. Newcastle upon Tyne: Cambridge Scholars Press, pp. 45–56.

Sounes, Howard (2007) *Seventies: The Sights, Sounds and Ideas of a Brilliant Decade*. London: Pocket Books.

Southern, Terry, and Michael Cooper (1966) *A Clockwork Orange* Screenplay, First Draft, August, SK/13/1/1, SKA.

Southern, Terry (1970/1996) *Blue Movie*. New York: Grove. (Originally published by New American Library in 1970.)

Southworth, June (1972) 'Cinema Violence Renews Yobs' Faith in Bovver Power', *Doncaster Gazette and Chronicle*, 27 January, unpaginated clipping in SK/13/6/30, vol. 1, SKA.

Spence, Rob (2009) 'Hogg, Hoggart and the Uses of Illiteracy: Anthony Burgess and Pop Music', in Marc Jeannin (ed.) *Anthony Burgess: Music in Literature and Literature in Music*. Newcastle upon Tyne: Cambridge Scholars Press, pp. 37–43.

Sperb, Jason (2006) *The Kubrick Facade: Faces and Voices in the Films of Stanley Kubrick*. Lanham, MD: Scarecrow Press.

Springfield Republican (1963) Review of *A Clockwork Orange*, 13 January, unpaginated clipping in SK/13/6/29/45, SKA.

Springhall, John (1998) *Youth, Popular Culture and Moral Panics: Penny Gaffs to Gangsta-Rap, 1830–1996*. Basingstoke: Macmillan.

Staiger, Janet (2003) 'The Cultural Productions of *A Clockwork Orange*', in Stuart Y. McDougal (ed.) *Stanley Kubrick's* A Clockwork Orange. Cambridge: Cambridge University Press, pp. 37–60.

Staiger, Janet (2005) *Media Reception Studies*. New York: New York University Press.

Stanley, Donald (1963) 'Grim Social Satire', *San Francisco Examiner*, 17 January, unpaginated clipping in folder SK/13/6/29/45, SKA.

Steinberg, Cobbett S. (1980) *Film Facts*. New York: Facts on File.

Steinhorn, Leonard (2006) *The Greater Generation: In Defense of the Baby Boom Legacy*. New York: Thomas Dunne.

Stoddart, Patrick (1973) 'Why Bovver Boys Like the Glitter', *Evening News* (London), 17 January, unpaginated clipping in SK/13/6/30, vol. 3, SKA.

Stratton, Jon (1985/1997) 'On the Importance of Subcultural Origins', extract from 'Youth Subcultures and Their Cultural Contexts', *Australian and New Zealand Journal of*

Sociology vol. 21 no. 2, reprinted in Ken Gelder and Sarah Thornton (eds) *The Subcultures Reader*. London: Routledge, pp. 181–90.

Stratton, Jon (1996) 'Serial Killing and the Transformation of the Social', *Theory, Culture and Society* vol. 13 no. 1, February, pp. 77–98.

Streatfeild, Dominic (2007) *Brainwash: The Secret History of Mind Control*. London: Hodder.

Strick, Philip (1971/72) 'Kubrick's Horrorshow', *Sight and Sound*, Winter, pp. 45–6.

Strick, Philip, and Penelope Houston (1972/2001) 'Modern Times: An Interview with Stanley Kubrick', *Sight and Sound*, Spring 1972, reprinted in Gene D. Phillips (ed.) *Stanley Kubrick: Interviews*. Jackson: University Press of Mississippi, pp. 126–39.

Stubbs, Jonathan (2007) *Inventing England: Representations of English History in Hollywood Cinema*, unpublished PhD dissertation, University of East Anglia.

The Sun (1972) 'The Rising Tide of Violence', 7 January, pp. 16–17.

Surgeon General's Scientific Advisory Committee on Television and Social Behavior (1972) *Television and Growing Up: The Impact of Televised Violence*. Washington, DC: US Government Printing Office.

Talbot, Daniel (1963) Review of *A Clockwork Orange*, *New York Herald-Tribune*, 14 April, p. 7.

Taylor, Greg (1999) *Artists in the Audience: Cults, Camp, and American Film Criticism*. Princeton, NJ: Princeton University Press.

Taylor, Ian, and Dave Wall (1976) 'Beyond the Skinheads: Comments on the Emergence and Significance of the Glamrock Cult', in Geoff Mungham and Geoff Pearson (eds) *Working Class Youth Culture*. London: Routledge and Kegan Paul, pp. 105–23.

Taylor, Kathleen (2004) *Brainwashing: The Science of Thought Control*. Oxford: Oxford University Press.

Taylor, Kathleen (2009) *Cruelty: Human Evil and the Human Brain*. Oxford: Oxford University Press.

Telotte, J. P. (2001) *Science Fiction Film*. Cambridge: Cambridge University Press.

Thorpe, Dan (1963) 'A New Comic Novel, in Strange, New Words', *Star* (Washington, DC), 3 March, unpaginated clipping in SK/13/6/29/45, SKA.

The Times (London) (1973) '*A Clockwork Orange*', 18 January, unpaginated clipping on Stanley Kubrick fiche, AMPAS.

Travis, Alan (1999) 'Retake on Kubrick Film Ban', *Guardian*, 11 September, p. 3.

Trend, David (2007) *The Myth of Media Violence: A Critical Introduction*. Malden, MA: Blackwell.

Trevelyan, John (1973) *What the Censor Saw*. London: Michael Joseph.

Tropiani, Stephen (2009) *Obscene, Indecent, Immoral, and Offensive: 100+ Years of Censored, Banned, and Controversial Films*. New York: Limelight Editions.

Tucker, Martin (1963) 'Burgess Comes of Age', *Courier-Journal*, 6 January, Section 4, p. 5.

Turner, Alwyn W. (2008) *Crisis? What Crisis? Britain in the 1970s*. London: Aurum Press.

Valenti, Jack (2007) *This Time, This Place: My Life in War, the White House, and Hollywood*. New York: Three Rivers Press.

Variety (1966) 'All-Time Top Grossers', 5 January, pp. 6, 36, 72.

Variety (1970) 'Kubrick Will Make *Clockwork* for WB', 3 February, unpaginated clipping on the *Clockwork Orange* fiche, AMPAS.

Variety (1971) ' "X" for *Clockwork*: WB Must Accept "As Is" of Kubrick', 15 December, unpaginated clipping in the *Clockwork Orange* folder, PARC.

Variety (1972) 'Bouquets and Brickbats for Kubrick's *Orange* from British Critics', 19 January, unpaginated clipping on the Stanley Kubrick fiche, AMPAS.

Variety (1974) 'Think *Orange* Took $2,500,000 in Gt. Britain', 16 January, unpaginated clipping on the Stanley Kubrick fiche, AMPAS.

Variety (1980) '*Orange* Added to WCI Home Video Catalog', 27 September, unpaginated clipping on *A Clockwork Orange* fiche, AMPAS.

Vaughn, Stephen (2006) *Freedom and Entertainment: Rating the Movies in an Age of New Media*. Cambridge: Cambridge University Press.

Waddington, P. A. J. (1986) 'Mugging as a Moral Panic: A Question of Proportion', *British Journal of Sociology* vol. 37 no. 2, June, pp. 245–59.

Walker, Alexander (1972a) 'Violence Comes of Age', *Evening Standard*, 28 December, unpaginated clipping in SK/13/6/30, vol. 3, SKA.

Walker, Alexander (1972b) 'A Bit of the Old Ultra-violence', *Evening Standard*, 13 January 1972, unpaginated clipping in SK/13/6/30, vol. 1, SKA.

Walker, Alexander (1972c) *Stanley Kubrick Directs*. New York: Harcourt Brace.

Walker, Alexander, Sybil Taylor and Ulrich Ruchti (1999) *Stanley Kubrick, Director: A Visual Analysis*. New York: W. W. Norton.

Walker, Beverly (1972) 'From Novel to Film: Kubrick's *A Clockwork Orange*', *Women and Film* vol. 2, pp. 4–10.

Wallis, Roy (1976) 'Moral Indignation and the Media: An Analysis of NVALA', *Sociology* vol. 10, pp. 271–95.

Walsh, Frank (1996) *Sin and Censorship: The Catholic Church and the Motion Picture Industry*. New Haven, CT: Yale University Press.

Warner Bros. (1972) *A Clockwork Orange* press book, author's collection.

Warner Bros. (1973) 'No Cuts in *Clockwork Orange*', Warner Bros. press release, dated 4 January, SK/13/6/30, vol. 3, SKA.

Warner Bros. (1982) 'Stanley Kubrick's *A Clockwork Orange* Set for February 12 Re-release by Warner Bros.', 9 February, press release on *A Clockwork Orange* fiche, AMPAS.

Watson, Albert (1972) 'For the First Time I Say "Cut" ', *Evening Post* (Reading), 24 January, unpaginated clipping in SK/13/6/30, vol. 1, SKA.

Watson, Steve (2003) *Factory Made: The Warhol Sixties*. New York: Pantheon.

Weiler, A. H. (1970) 'Kubrick to Adapt *A Clockwork Orange*', *New York Times*, 3 February, unpaginated clipping in folder MFL+n.c.2247, PARC.

Weinraub, Bernard (1972) 'Kubrick Tells What Makes *Clockwork Orange* Tick', *New York Times*, 4 January, unpaginated clipping on Stanley Kubrick fiche, AMPAS.

West, Mark I. (1988) *Children, Culture, and Controversy*. Hamden, CT: Archon.

Whitehouse, Mary (1996) 'Time to Face Responsibility', in Karl French (ed.) *Screen Violence*. London: Bloomsbury, pp. 52–61.

Willetts, Paul (2010) *Members Only: The Life and Times of Paul Raymond*. London: Serpent's Tail.

Williams, Linda (2008) *Screening Sex*. Durham, NC: Duke University Press.

Winchell, Mark Royden (2008) *God, Man and Hollywood: Politically Incorrect Cinema from* The Birth of a Nation *to* The Passion of the Christ. Wilmington, DE: JSJ Books.

Wittern-Keller, Laura (2008) *Freedom of the Screen: Legal Challenges to State Film Censorship, 1915–1981*. Lexington: University Press of Kentucky.

Wyatt, Justin (2000) 'The Stigma of X: Adult Cinema and the Institution of the MPAA Ratings System', in Matthew Bernstein (ed.) *Controlling Hollywood: Censorship and Regulation in the Studio Era*. London: Athlone Press, pp. 238–63.

Yankelovich, Daniel (1974) *The New Morality: A Profile of American Youth in the 70s*. New York: McGraw-Hill.

Yeiser, Frederick (1963) 'There's Moral Fable in New Language', *Cincinnati Enquirer*, 26 January, unpaginated clipping in SK/13/6/29/45, SKA.

Yudkin, Vivian (1963) 'Novel of the Week: Pleasure Found in Violence', *Washington Post*, 13 January, unpaginated clipping in SK/13/6/29/45, SKA.

Zillmann, Dolf (1998) 'The Psychology of the Appeal of Portrayals of Violence', in Jeffrey H. Goldstein (ed.) *Why We Watch: The Attractions of Violent Entertainment*. New York: Oxford University Press, pp. 179–211.

Zimmerman, Paul D. (1972) 'Kubrick's Brilliant Vision', *Newsweek*, 3 January, pp. 28–33.

Zotigh, Barbara (1963) 'Satiric Tale of Hoodlums', *Tulsa World*, 17 February, unpaginated clipping in SK/13/6/29/45, SKA.

Index

Page numbers in **bold** denote extended/detailed treatment; those in *italic* refer to illustrations.